Charlotte Hawkins Brown

One Woman's Dream

Charlotte Hawkins Brown

One Woman's Dream

Diane Silcox-Jarrett

Winston-Salem, North Carolina

Library of Congress Catalog Card Number 95-80963

ISBN 1-878177-07-9

Bandit Books, Inc.

P.O. Box 11721

Winston-Salem, NC 27116-1721

(910) 785-7417

Cover design by Lynn Mann

Cover photograph courtesy of the N.C. Division of Archives and History

To Alex and Daniel
with all my love

Charlotte Hawkins Brown
Courtesy of the N.C. Division of Archives and History

TABLE OF CONTENTS

Acknowledgments

I would like to thank the following:

Charles Wadelington, who gave a tremendous amount of his time and knowledge to this project, for always sharing his wonderful sense of humor.

Ruth Totten, who first introduced Charlotte Hawkins Brown to me and shared her extraordinary stories of the woman and Palmer Institute.

Laurie Green and Anita Nevils, who spent many hours editing this project from the moment I started on it. Jennifer Weston, Gail Chesson, and June Eason for their editing.

My publisher, Barry McGee, who shared his ideas and insight on the book and spent many hours editing.

Lynn Mann, who shared her artistic talent on the cover.

Lee Smith for her suggestions and support.

Alumni and friends of Palmer Institute and Charlotte Hawkins Brown for sharing their memories. Without their help and stories this book would never have been completed.

The Division of Archives and History, North Carolina Historic Sites, who let us use their photographs for the book.

Gina Goldwater for her encouragement.

My sister, Sharon, and my father, Harry, for their support.

All my friends who supported me when I decided to stay home with my son and pursue my writing.

My son, Daniel, who somehow took a nap when I needed to write.

My husband, Alex, who believed in me and this project from the moment we met Ruth Totten at the Charlotte Hawkins Brown State Historic Site, one summer day, five years ago.

Introduction

I was first introduced to Charlotte Hawkins Brown one July day in 1990. My husband and I were driving up Interstate 85 toward a vacation in the mountains. As we neared Burlington, North Carolina, I saw the signs for the Charlotte Hawkins Brown Memorial State Historic Site. I had attended Elon College, only a few miles from there, and had passed by the empty buildings many times. Though I had wondered what happened there, I'd never stopped. On that July day, heading for our vacation, I decided to finally learn the story behind those big, empty buildings.

When we arrived, we were greeted by Ruth Totten, who had taught and lived in those buildings when they were known as Palmer Institute. She had a wonderful talent for recreating the days when Palmer was full of students and led by a strong, determined woman. She told us of dances, and of dresses flown in specially for those dances. She told us of the respect received by Charlotte Hawkins Brown from fellow educators and presidents of the United States. She told us of students seeing movies in Greensboro, and having to sit in the balcony. She told us of Palmer graduates who had learned their school work, but also learned how to act like ladies and gentlemen. She told us of a woman that other people needed to hear about.

I decided right then to write a book about Charlotte Hawkins Brown.

When I returned to my home in Raleigh, I contacted Charles Wadelington of the North Carolina State Historic Sites. I quickly discovered he was the authority on Charlotte Hawkins Brown. With his guidance and assistance I began writing.

The most enjoyable part of my research was talking to the friends of Charlotte Hawkins Brown, and the former teachers and alumni of Palmer Institute. I know I will probably never again have the chance to associate with so many fascinating people. Palmer graduates are in a class by themselves. They are genuine, poised people who carry a deep respect for the woman that taught them to be that way. I took their stories and memories and wove them into this book.

This book is a creative nonfiction piece, based on fact with the creative part coming into the development of particular scenes. I used this approach so the reader could experience Charlotte the way I experienced her through the stories. I wish I could have recreated all the stories I heard. And I wish I had heard even more stories.

Charlotte Hawkins Brown was truly an unique woman, especially for the time in which she lived. I regret that I never got to meet her or have even a single conversation with her. I learned from others that she was a strong educator, leader, and advocate for human rights, but she never forgot to take care of the little things in life that mean so much, like listening to a student's dreams.

I hope you, the reader, will get to know Charlotte as I did. A woman who dreamed of touching hundreds of lives and making a real difference in them. A woman who saw her dream come true.

One

Charlotte's Determination

Charlotte was determined to have a silk slip like all the other girls at her high school graduation, despite what her mother thought. She couldn't think of a single reason why she should be the only girl not wearing one. Her white dress would look so pretty, like the others, but it wouldn't be the same without the smooth, cool, silk slip against her skin.

Whenever she went downtown to the store, she always stopped by the ladies' clothing and looked at the silk slips. They were neatly tucked away in glass cases, stacked separately in three colors: light blue, light pink, and white. Dainty white lace had been sewn across the front of each one. Charlotte looked at them, touching the glass over the slips, wanting to feel the material. Once a saleslady saw her and asked if she would like to see one. Charlotte said yes and lightly rubbed her finger tips over the soft fabric.

As Charlotte sat at the desk in her bedroom, working on her English homework, the spring breeze from the harbor in Cambridge, Massachusetts blew in the window and cooled her. Cool, smooth—and once again her thoughts returned to a silk slip. The breeze carried in the scent of her mother's newly blooming roses, and Charlotte thought of the corsages all the girls would wear on graduation day. She wanted one made with the velvety pink roses that bloomed by the gate in the backyard. She sighed; there wasn't time now to think about slips or roses. She had to finish writing her paper.

She had worked hard through high school. Even though she loved her classes, there were times when she would rather have gone to the park or off to laugh and talk with her friends. But education was important to her mother, and Charlotte wanted to do her best.

If only her mother could understand how much she wanted a silk slip.

I have to have a slip, Charlotte thought. I just have to. She pictured herself getting ready for the big day. The slip would slide over her body, wrapping her in smoothness. All her family would wait for her downstairs. She could see herself, walking slowly down the stairs, wearing her fine white dress, her hair fixed up in a bun with her mother's favorite combs. And underneath, where no one could see, was her silk slip. Charlotte closed her eyes and smiled. She saw herself with her friends, standing ready to receive her diploma, waiting for the most important moment of her life.

"Why would you want to spend so much on a silly slip?" her mother had asked her earlier that afternoon. Obviously she had not been in a mood to listen to Charlotte's problem. Her mother didn't even raise her head when she spoke. "You're being vain, Charlotte, and you know that is not becoming in a young lady."

The words stuck in Charlotte. "I'm not vain," she told herself, though she stepped in front of the mirror to look for signs of vanity. She saw none. How could she be vain? She wasn't as pretty as a lot of the girls in her class, but she was petite and carried herself well.

"You have a strong face," her mother told her. "You have determination in your eyes."

Charlotte sighed. Petite with determination, she thought. I guess there could be worse combinations. "I just want to be among the best, Mother," she answered. Her mother had just smiled before she walked out of the room.

Her mother hadn't understood at all. Charlotte stopped working on her homework, rose from her desk, and looked in the mirror again. She patted her hair into place. Maybe a hat with spring flowers all over it would give her a softer look. Yes, a hat would be nice for graduation.

It looks like I'll have to find a way to buy my own slip, Charlotte thought. I'll get a part-time job and save enough money. Maybe I'll even have enough left over to buy a hat, too. She took one last look in the mirror, noticing that her dark brown eyes sparkled. "I'll have the finest slip and hat on graduation day," she said aloud.

Charlotte went out the next day and found a job baby-sitting two children in her neighborhood. She earned three dollars and fifty cents a week. Her hard work paid off. Not only did she make enough money for the slip, she had enough to buy her own hat.

She held herself straight and proud, and smiled throughout her graduation exercise.

Two years later Charlotte would have to muster this same type of determination, but this time it would not just help her. Thousands of people for years to come would learn of Charlotte's strong will, and benefit from it.

*   *   *

Charlotte Hawkins Brown was born on June 11, 1883, as Lottie Hawkins in Henderson, North Carolina. Just before she graduated from high school, she decided her name was not elegant enough, and changed it to Charlotte Eugenia Hawkins.

Her mother was Caroline Frances Hawkins (many people called her Carrie), her father was Edmund H. Heght. Her mother was a direct descendant of the English navigator, John D. Hawkins, whose children settled in Vance County, North Carolina.

Charlotte was born in a house located where part of the Hawkins plantation had once been. The house had four large columns on the front and was one of the finest homes owned by an African-American family in Henderson. Charlotte lived with her family among reproductions of famous paintings. White ruffled curtains hung throughout the house, and everywhere were decorations with rainbow colors of blooms from the flower garden. A hand-pump organ, which no one could play, sat on display in the hallway because her mother felt it showed the family had good taste.

One of the main things that Charlotte learned while growing up was how to act in public. At the age of three she gave her first speech. Her mother dressed her in a stiff starched dress, and tied blue ribbons in her hair. Then she stood Charlotte on the settee to recite, "Suffer the little children to come unto Me, and forbid them not, for of such is the Kingdom of Heaven."

Mrs. Hawkins had received her education from the Elementary Department of Shaw University in Raleigh, North Carolina. She wanted her children to become well educated and experience all the best life could offer.

At this time in the South–and also in the North, though less frequently–there were many Jim Crow laws. Beginning in the 1880s, these laws were established to keep blacks and whites separated. The name, Jim Crow, came from an African-American character in a popular song of the 1830s. The laws prevented African-American girls and boys from attending the same schools as white children, or even sitting together on the same trains. Mrs. Hawkins hated the laws, and did not want her children to grow up in this type of atmosphere. She knew that people in New England were not as conservative in their thinking toward blacks, and that her children could receive a better education there. Charlotte's mother felt there was a better life for her children in the North, so the family packed up their belongings and left their nice home and farm in North Carolina. Charlotte was five years old.

The family's move to Cambridge in 1888 not only included Charlotte's immediate family, but also several uncles, aunts, and cousins. Mrs. Hawkins had divorced Charlotte's father and married a man named Nelson Willis.

The family traveled by train to Norfolk, Virginia, where they were to board a boat. "My brother, my younger aunts, and I were told that a boat bigger than the house in which we lived would take us to Boston," Charlotte wrote later. She had never been out of her home town, and the adventure of moving made her heart beat faster. When she saw the ocean for the first time, it looked too big to believe, stretching on and on without end. Strange smells filled the air, the salt, the water, the fish. The boat, anchored in the harbor, rocked back and forth as the waves slapped its wooden sides. Every few moments the boat made a creaking noise. Charlotte felt spellbound as her senses tried to take in everything, and hardly noticed when her mother grabbed her hand to get on board.

The seagulls' loud screeches made Charlotte jump as she started up the ramp. She remembered some things she had been told, decided the boat didn't look safe, and stopped. "I'm afraid," she told her mother. "I'm afraid of those big sea monsters out there in the water. Will they eat me up on the boat?"

"Charlotte, who ever told you such a thing? Have your cousins been teasing you?" Her mother smiled and gathered Charlotte up in her arms. Charlotte gladly snuggled closer to her mother. She smelled the vanilla extract her mother wore, a scent that reminded her of her old home. Charlotte's stomach tightened thinking about getting on board the boat.

"There's no such things as sea monsters," her mother said gently. "The ocean is only full of wonderful things like star fish. I'll tell you all about them on our trip." She put Charlotte down, and together they stepped onto the boat.

The voyage took several days. Their cabins on the boat were down in the center. Because they were African-Americans, Charlotte's family ate in a separate area in the dining room, or at a different time than the white passengers. The boat made the journey North safely, and the family settled in Cambridge, Massachusetts.

All the new sights overwhelmed Charlotte. Everyone always seemed to be in such a hurry. She had never seen so many people in one place with so many things to do; they rushed in and out of stores, shopping or doing business. Everyone talked faster there, and sometimes she couldn't understand what they said. She would just nod her head and smile. The smells were different, too. A faint odor of fish and wet wood filled the city. Charlotte knew she would miss the sweet smell of the magnolia blossoms in the spring.

There were so many new learning experiences for Charlotte in Cambridge that soon all her days were full, leaving no time to think of what she had left behind.

Mr. Willis worked as a janitor and at other jobs. Charlotte's mother also supported the family by operating a hand laundry. Charlotte helped by making deliveries and ironing fancy handkerchiefs. She had to be careful as she ironed each delicate piece. The heavy, hot iron she pulled out of the fire would scorch the fine linen unless she handled it just right. She thought of the rich ladies living in Cambridge, and how each of them must have a fancy handkerchief. "It seems like some of them might even have dozens, as many as I have to iron. I know I'll never have such a silly accessory when I grow up," she said.

Charlotte's family boarded black male Harvard students. Their home was known for its hospitality, and African-American scholars from all parts of the country stayed there.

Charlotte grew to love her new home, and took advantage of the opportunities she had there. Her first years at school were spent at Allston Grammar School in Cambridge. Among her friends were Alice and Edith Longfellow, the daughters of Henry Wadsworth Longfellow. Charlotte enjoyed learning and became known for her talents in drama and art. She loved teaching. At age twelve she organized her church's kindergarten department.

Her church provided many other projects for Charlotte. When the minister celebrated his fifteenth year in the ministry, he asked Charlotte, at age fourteen, to speak at the ceremony. Nervous, but excited about her opportunity, she spoke in front of a large crowd that included the governor of Massachusetts and his council. One of the dignitaries who attended remarked, "I expect to hear from that girl in the future."

Growing up in an urban New England community, Charlotte saw that it was possible for people of all races to live and work together.

One Christmas season she stood in the department store downtown, considering if some beautiful silk scarves would be a good present for her mother. While she was deciding, carolers began to sing. Charlotte walked over to the singers, who stood in the center of the store. They had dressed in red and white, and stood on a balcony with a background painting of the Madonna and child. The director asked the crowd to join the singers in "O Come All Ye Faithful." Everyone sang.

"There were gray-haired women, the ragged, the poor and little children," Charlotte wrote later.

A Quaker woman standing next to Charlotte offered to share her song book. She said, "Let us sing together; that is what Christmas is all about. That is the way it should be all year. No matter what. We all should sing together."

Charlotte looked into the woman's light blue eyes and smiled as she joined in singing. Snow fell outside. The sweet smell of chocolate from the next counter drifted through the store. A warm feeling went all through Charlotte.

"Why can't everyone feel like this?" she wondered.

Two

Decision of a Lifetime

"We'll go back and play on the swings in the park in a little while!" Charlotte said with more pleading in her voice than she wanted. The two children she was baby-sitting were basically sweet, but they demanded every bit of Charlotte's attention. She had played with toy boats in the pond and fed ducks all morning. It was a beautiful day. It seemed as if everyone in Cambridge had come out to enjoy the spring weather. Everywhere parents and children played, and couples walked, hand-in-hand. Crocuses and daffodils dotted the streets with their white and yellow blossoms bouncing in the wind. Charlotte had decided to leave the park to go for a short walk down the street, but the baby became restless. The baby's four year-old brother, Joseph, had asked an endless stream of questions all morning. He loved seeing the kites, dotting the sky with their bright colors.

"How do they stay up in the sky, Charlotte?" he asked.

"The wind keeps them up," she answered.

"But how does the wind keep them up?"

She didn't feel like giving him a long scientific explanation. "God breathes real gently like this." Charlotte blew softly into one of her hands. "And that's what keeps them up. God enjoys seeing all the bright colors, too."

Joseph smiled at her, satisfied with the answer.

The baby, a six month-old girl, started crying. "Come on, Joseph," Charlotte said. "Let's finish our walk and see if I can get Anna calmed down." Joseph fell in behind her. As they walked, Charlotte took out her book of poetry by the Latin author Virgil and started reading. Lost in the words, she didn't notice a poised lady coming toward her.

"It's so unusual to see someone of your age reading such a difficult piece of literature," the lady said.

Startled, Charlotte looked up to find a well-dressed woman smiling down at her. She wore a long skirt and buttoned-up shoes that made her look tall. Or maybe she looked so tall because Charlotte herself was small, or maybe it was because the woman had an air of importance about her. Charlotte couldn't decide before the woman spoke again.

"I didn't mean to interrupt your reading, but I was so impressed with your reading selection. Let me introduce myself. I'm Alice Freeman Palmer." The woman smiled at Charlotte. Her ruffled blouse came right up under her chin, and soft black curls touched the bottom of her collar. She reached down to pat Joseph's head. The woman captivated Charlotte.

"I just got this the other day and haven't had a chance to read it," Charlotte said. "I thought the fresh air would keep my head clear enough so I could concentrate on it. My teacher recommended Virgil to me."

"You have a very wise teacher," Mrs. Palmer said. "What is your name?"

"Charlotte Hawkins." Charlotte looked down, embarrassed; she had forgotten her manners.

"Well, Miss Hawkins, you and I will have to be sure and talk sometime again. I'm always interested in bright, young people," Mrs. Palmer said. "I'll leave you alone with your book."

As Mrs. Palmer walked away, Charlotte noticed how straight she held herself, how she glided down the street. Charlotte didn't realize that she had met a great humanitarian and the first woman president of Wellesley College, located near Boston. She also couldn't realize the impact Alice Freeman Palmer would have on her future. It began as a simple introduction on a sunny day and it would grow into a friendship that lasted until Alice's death.

*   *   *

When Charlotte graduated from high school, she wanted to attend college. Her mother had other ideas and told her, "You have a good high school education, good background and character, and with a little political pull you could get a teaching appointment in the schools of Massachusetts."

But Charlotte knew where her dreams lay. She wanted to graduate from college first, then become a teacher. While looking through the brochures for the State Normal School in Salem, she saw that Alice Freeman Palmer was on the board of directors. She remembered the lady she had met the day she was baby-sitting, and hoped Mrs. Palmer remembered her. Charlotte wrote to Palmer about her problem with her mother. She said that when she was young she heard her mother praying upstairs, asking God to help Charlotte fulfill her dreams. Charlotte had vowed right then never to disappoint her mother. She told Mrs. Palmer that she felt ready to fulfill her dreams, but her mother didn't understand how she planned to accomplish it.

Once again, Charlotte's desire to learn impressed Alice Freeman Palmer. She helped Charlotte start her education at the two-year State Normal School at Salem by paying part of the tuition. Young Charlotte returned the favor by working hard. She visited Mrs. Palmer often, and they spent hours talking of books and dreams and helping others.

Charlotte took an eighteen-mile trolley ride to Salem each day. The trolley tracks were designed for city to city traveling, which had come to be called interurban train travel. Trolleys became popular after the Civil War, since they could be used to connect small towns together. The trolleys were built of wood, and painted black, red, and green. The seats were wooden benches that ran down the middle of the car. Most of the room was for standing. The adventurous person could even hang on the outside of the trolley for short trips. Trains moved slowly in 1900 when Charlotte started at the State Normal School. The trip took one hour each way.

While the Massachusetts landscape passed by, Charlotte read over class assignments. The ride was bumpy, and sometimes the rhythm of the train on the tracks made it hard for her to read the jumping words on the page. So many interesting people rode the trolley, and they all seemed to be in such a hurry to get to their destination. Charlotte watched them, often making up little stories about them in her mind.

On one of these long rides, Charlotte met a woman who offered her a lifetime challenge. While riding back to Cambridge one afternoon, she met Mrs. Emerson, field secretary of the American Missionary Association. This religious organization supported African-American education in the South after the Civil War. Charlotte listened intently as Mrs. Emerson explained the organization's work and goals. Already influenced by the progressive thinking in New England, Charlotte vowed to return to the South to help African-Americans who hadn't had the same opportunities she had. Mrs. Emerson told Charlotte about two jobs, one at an already established school in Florida, and the other at a one-room school house in North Carolina.

When Charlotte got home that night, she told her mother of the woman she had met and the need for teachers in the South.

"But you wanted to finish college, Charlotte," her mother said, though she must have known from the excitement in her daughter's face that her words were useless. "You're the one who wanted that so badly."

"I know I did," Charlotte said, "but you've always taught me that we have to help those less fortunate than us. We always learn in church how blacks in the South are not receiving an education and we must help them."

Charlotte pictured all the great women who were making an impact on the future of her race. She thought of Catherine Beecher who had founded Western Female Institution in Cincinnati, Ohio, and Lucy Craft Laney who had founded the Haines Industrial Institute in Augusta, Georgia. The person's footsteps she most wanted to follow was Alice Palmer, her advisor and guide, the woman whose experience and wisdom Charlotte valued most in making decisions. Mrs. Palmer and the other women made Charlotte want to help the people of her race gain the education and chances in life they deserved.

Charlotte looked at her mother. "I feel a need to teach in the South." She knew in her heart that her mother wouldn't go against her desire. "This would be my opportunity to make a difference and maybe help some people reach their dreams."

"I won't stop you, Charlotte," her mother said as she put her arm around her daughter. "I just pray to God you have made the right choice."

Charlotte Hawkins in 1905
Courtesy of N.C. State Historic Sites

Three

Arrival in the South

Charlotte hadn't realized she had dozed off until she heard the conductor yell, "McLeansville stop, anybody getting off better hurry." When she fell asleep she had been trying to remember what the South was like when she was a young girl. The summers will be hotter and the winters will be milder, she thought. It had been many years since her family took the train trip from Henderson to Norfolk, and then boarded the boat for Boston. Now she was returning without the companionship of her family or a single friend. She was returning alone to a South she knew very little about.

It had taken two long, miserable days to make the trip. Charlotte's back ached, and she didn't know how much longer she could stand the smell of the coal from the burners. Since Charlotte made her trip in August, the windows of the train stayed open so there would be a little breeze, but she found that everything else in the world came through those windows—plenty of flies, dust, dirt, and smoke. She wore the same garment as the other passengers, a wrap that looked like a cloak to keep the dirt off her clothes. She rode with the other African-Americans in a separate car from the whites, a car located close to the locomotive, which made for an even more unpleasant ride, especially in the summer. If she could survive the trip, at least the American Missionary Association had told someone to meet her at the train stop.

When the conductor announced McLeansville, Charlotte panicked. She thought, I was supposed to get off at Sedalia. She noticed no one else rose to get off. She asked the conductor why the train stopped here, since she saw nothing but woods out there. The conductor told her that this was as close to Sedalia as the train would get. He pointed out the window. "Just walk that dirt path, Miss," he said. "That will take you straight to Sedalia."

Charlotte grabbed the rail, ready to swing down to the ground as soon as the train stopped. It kept rolling. She hesitated. "You better jump, Miss," the conductor yelled. He threw her luggage out onto the ground. "This train is not stopping." Charlotte let go of the rail and jumped. The ground rushed at her and she stumbled, almost falling over her luggage. What a way to arrive! She stood and watched the train disappear down the track, then looked around her. Surely someone had come out to meet the new school teacher—the American Missionary Association said they would—but she saw no one. Didn't they know she was coming today? Charlotte sighed. She coughed out the smoke from the train, dusted off her clothes, and picked up her luggage. The air around her felt like a hazy and humid blanket, something she wasn't at all used to. Some black-eyed susans bloomed in the tall grass beside the train track, the only thing around to greet Charlotte to her new home.

She chose a direction on the dirt path and started walking, hoping she had gone the right way. Two white men eyed her, none too friendly, as she neared and then passed them. Charlotte felt empty and alone. She wiped the sweat off her forehead, noticed the tips of her shoes were covered with dust. The blouse of her gray suit scratched her back, and her long skirt weighed heavy around her waist.

A young white couple, holding hands, walked toward her. Charlotte started to ask them if they knew the way to the school. I'll have to remember to be tactful, she thought, knowing that whites' attitudes toward blacks were far different in the South than the North.

The young couple had never heard of the school, but told Charlotte that she could follow them and maybe meet someone on the way who had heard of Bethany Institute.

As she walked behind the couple, Charlotte's stomach grew tighter. She didn't know if it was from hunger or the fact that she was completely lost in what now looked to be endless farmland. She couldn't believe the difference between this land and her Cambridge home. The fields stretched on for miles, filled with old tobacco and corn leaves that had faded to yellow and brown. The plants waved gently in the wind, as if they waited patiently to be plowed under. The sounds of insects filled Charlotte's ears. Their loudness amazed her as they sang in a constant, squeaky chorus. I'm a long, long way from home, she thought, as she watched a flock of crows pass over her head.

Charlotte later wrote about her arrival in North Carolina: "No one seemed to be expecting me, so I had to find my way alone. I cannot forget that moment, for I felt as though I wanted to go back home. I did not then know, as I now do, that God knew what was best for me. I wanted to enter His service, but had not thought of entering such a barren field. However, after thinking over my desire, I said, 'This is God's way; I must be satisfied.'"

Still following the young couple through the farmland, Charlotte heard a sad, sweet sound over the insects. The sound had a soothing melody to it, and she recognized it was a woman's voice. Charlotte looked toward the voice, and saw a black woman walking through one of the fields.

What a lovely voice, Charlotte thought. A friendly voice. As the woman came closer, Charlotte saw she was a young woman, not much older than herself. The woman stood very tall, but her shoulders stooped. Charlotte told the young couple to go on without her, since she wanted to talk to the woman. She walked off in the direction of the sweet-sounding voice, and finally caught up with the woman.

"Hello, I'm Charlotte Hawkins, the new school teacher at Bethany Institute." Charlotte held out her hand.

The woman eyed her up and down, stopping at the cameo brooch Charlotte's mother had given her. "You sure are dressed up to be walking in a field," she said, putting down the bucket of peas she carried. "You look like you're ready to go Sunday visiting."

"I just got off the train and didn't know which way to go to find the school," Charlotte answered. "I heard your beautiful voice and thought you might be able to tell me which way to go."

The woman smiled at Charlotte's compliment. "I sure do know the way to the school. My son, Jacob, goes there from time to time. You know, he has to help us in the fields whenever he can. I know schooling is important, but a family has to eat, too."

She took off her straw hat. Her soaked hair revealed how much the woman had been sweating. Her pink and white dress looked worn around the bottom, but it had lace trim sewn around the neck and sleeves. The lace reminded Charlotte of the hundreds of handkerchiefs she had ironed as a child. She wished she had a handkerchief to give the woman.

"I tell you what," the woman said with a smile. "Why don't you come with me and I'll get my husband to take you over to the school. I don't live far from here."

Charlotte's trip from Boston was coming to an end. Finally!

The woman's husband drove Charlotte to the school in a wagon pulled by mules. The sun was setting and the heat fading when the wagon pulled up to a small run-down church.

"Well, this is it," the man said, pointing to the old building. "The Reverend Baldwin should be around somewhere. He lives over there, in that house next to the church."

Charlotte stepped down from the wagon and thanked the man for the ride. She told him she looked forward to seeing his son, Jacob, at the school. He waved and drove slowly off. Once again Charlotte heard the loud noise of the insects, but now their chorus had a different tone, as if they were warning her, telling her to go back to Massachusetts. The evening shadows gave the building a lonely and empty look, much like the way Charlotte felt as she stood in the unkempt yard. She summoned the last of her tired courage and walked toward the house to announce her arrival.

A tall man opened the door. "I'm Charlotte Hawkins." The man's forehead crinkled. "The new school teacher," Charlotte added. She felt her patience fading. She just wanted to rest somewhere.

"So you're the new teacher," the man answered, still with a unbelieving look in his eyes.

"Yes. Didn't they tell you I was coming to teach, and what train I was on?"

"I did get a letter from the association," he said, his eyes carefully watching Charlotte. "But they never said what day you were coming."

"Well, I'm here, and I'm very tired." Every muscle in Charlotte's body ached. All she wanted to do was to lie down. I'm even too tired to look over my school house, she thought. "Could you please show me where I will be staying?"

Reverend Baldwin introduced himself and led Charlotte to her room, located in the loft of the church. Left alone, she looked at the straw-filled tick which was to be her bed, and thought about the cool crisp sheets that covered her bed in Cambridge. She closed her eyes and dreamed for a minute of her former home. By this time of evening there would be a breeze blowing through her window. She could almost feel that cool breeze across her face. That was another place, she thought as she opened her eyes and looked around the little room. She walked over to the window and looked up. She was amazed at how large the sky looked here, how many more stars she could see than up North. She longed to feel a breeze to cool her, but the air held still and the leaves did not move. Every place has its own special beauty, she thought as she collapsed on the bed.

Four

A Part of the Community

Charlotte's head throbbed as she sat down on the front pew of the church. She had just had a visit from several townspeople of Sedalia. Why did this have to happen? she thought. Just when everything was going so well. God must want me to prove how much I want to help my people here.

She had received a letter from the association saying they were closing all their one- and two-room school houses, and offering Charlotte a position somewhere else. Charlotte felt a tie to the people of this small community, even after these few months, and she felt they needed her, too. Who else would teach the children to read and learn the best way to run a farm? There were few high schools for whites, and none for African-Americans. Charlotte knew if she left, the children here would never get an education.

Charlotte looked out the window and remembered the first day of school in October when her first fifty students shyly walked into the church. Their expressions reflected a combination of fear and mistrust. Their clothes were worn and tattered, and many of them didn't fit. She smiled at them as they took their seats, hoping they couldn't tell how nervous she was. Charlotte knew in her heart she had to gain the children's trust first before the rest of the community would trust her. She also wanted the trust of the whites who lived there.

The whites in the community didn't trust Charlotte for three reasons: first, she was an African-American; second, she was a woman; and third, she came from up North. She had a better education than almost all of them. She had also come to teach African-Americans, which they thought would make blacks more dissatisfied with their lives. No one wanted trouble.

The African-Americans in the community felt suspicious of Charlotte's intentions and her way of life. The things she came to teach were strange and unfamiliar to them.

It took months of determination and hard work, but Charlotte finally gained the trust of her students and most of the community.

Charlotte noticed from the start that the children needed to be reassigned to classes. The ages of the students had little to do with their prior education, and therefore many were unsuited for the grade they were in. Charlotte placed the children in classes that best suited their educational level.

Then there was Mattie Nevils, the woman Charlotte had met in the field the first day she came to Sedalia. One Sunday after church, Mattie asked Charlotte if she could speak to her.

"Miss Hawkins," Mattie said, looking Charlotte straight in the eye, "I don't know how to read."

Charlotte waited to see what she would say next, but Mattie stood quietly, her lips pressed firmly together. Finally Charlotte asked, "Would you like me to teach you, Mattie?"

"Yes, Miss Hawkins," Mattie answered, breaking into a smile, "I sure would. Jacob is learning so much and I feel like I need to learn so I can help him. I want him to be something. I want him to be proud of me, too."

Charlotte and Mattie began meeting on Wednesday nights after church for half-hour lessons. Before the school year ended, Mattie could read just as well as her son.

All these things she had been through, and now–

Charlotte leaned forward and touched the window, the window of the school that she might never again get to look out it. I've worked hard for this, she thought. We all have worked hard for this. She remembered the long hours Reverend Baldwin put into the school. Every weekday they turned the community church into a school house with desks, books, and paper. They fought leaky roofs when it rained, and icy windows when it snowed. When the weather was hot, the room started out stuffy, and moved on to unbearable. The poor children sat there, sweating, fanning themselves with paper, and constantly asking for water.

On the coldest winter days, hardly anyone could make it to school. The ones that did would gather around the wood stove and try to keep warm. Charlotte taught them songs and hymns from her childhood to keep their minds off the cold. In turn, the children taught her old Negro spirituals. She smiled, thinking how badly they probably sounded, all of them singing off key, standing, shivering around the stove. Most of the children didn't have warm coats, and the holes in their shoes tore Charlotte's heart every time she looked at them. Still, even on the worst days, they had a good time while they learned about each other. As the year went on, they all grew closer.

I can't let these people down, Charlotte thought, looking around at the empty desks.

Vina and Emerson, two of Charlotte's students, were coming over that afternoon to help her pack up the books they had used all year. The two children lived nearby and helped Charlotte whenever they could. Vina had just turned fourteen, and Emerson was eight. Charlotte took a deep breath and straightened her dress, since she didn't want to let them see her upset. I have to let them think everything is going to be all right, she thought.

Charlotte had never gotten used to the musty smell of the church after it rained; it always made her feel closed in. She stepped outside and caught a whiff of the primrose that grew at the corner of the building.

The people of the community had begged her to stay. They had offered her all their support, but she knew it would take more than a few kind words. To make the school work it would take something the people of Sedalia didn't have—money.

Charlotte looked up to the light blue, cloudless sky. "What am I going to do?"

Just then Emerson and Vina came around the corner, smiling and carrying one of their grandmother's pies. Their mother had died several years before, and now they lived with their father and grandmother. When they first came to school, neither of them would talk to Charlotte, other than to say, "Yes, Miss Hawkins," or "No, Miss Hawkins." Charlotte soon learned all they needed was someone to show an interest in them. Both children learned fast and became two of her brightest students.

Vina wore the yellow cotton skirt Charlotte had helped her to make. They had spent many afternoons cutting the cloth and sewing. "I just can't do it," Vina said so many times, trying to make her hands twist the needle and thread.

"Yes, you can," Charlotte replied. She remembered when she was Vina's age how much trouble she had concentrating on sewing. "You'll get so good at this that one day we'll be sewing your wedding dress." Vina laughed, and went back to trying to thread the needle.

As she walked toward Charlotte now with Emerson, Vina stopped to pick some dandelions. As she stood back up, the wind caught Vina's skirt and lifted it. She reached down to keep it from going too far up her legs. She looked around to make sure no one had seen. Charlotte smiled. Vina's becoming a young lady, she thought. Somebody needs to be here to help her.

"Miss Hawkins, Miss Hawkins, guess what?" Emerson said. "Grandma made you one of her blueberry pies."

"Thank you so much!"

Charlotte took the pie and set it down as Emerson reached up to hug her. She leaned over and put her arms around the boy's small body. He smelled like the air of June and fresh cut hay. She squeezed him, and heard him giggle. And she made up her mind.

She was staying.

Charlotte's mind raced to all that lay ahead. Where would she get the money to run the school? Where would she find enough books? They needed more room for the students.

She was staying.

She let go of Emerson, smiled at his big brown eyes, and said, "Come on, let's get inside. There's a lot of work ahead for us."

Alice Freeman Palmer
Courtesy of N.C. State Historic Sites

Five

Raising Money

Charlotte had even more work in front of her than she imagined. She had planned to spend the summer of 1902 studying back in Salem, Massachusetts. Instead, she spent it raising funds for her school. Holding onto strong belief in herself, the people of Sedalia, and the school, she left for New England to raise money. She planned to make her small one-room school the best in the country.

On the train ride back to Massachusetts, Charlotte's mind poured over all she had to do and the short time she had to do it in. She had written Alice Palmer and told her what happened. She knew she could depend on Alice for help and guidance in her fund-raising efforts. Charlotte needed all of her friend's help that she could get.

*　*　*

Charlotte knocked lightly on the sitting room door at Alice Palmer's house. George, Alice's husband, had told Charlotte that his wife was taking a nap. The door stood ajar, but Charlotte couldn't tell if Alice was asleep.

"Come in."

Charlotte smiled at first, remembering her friend's voice, but there was something missing in it. When Charlotte opened the door all the way and entered the room, she knew immediately her friend wasn't well. Alice looked pale, even more pale than the rich peach covers of her couch. Still, she managed to smile and reach out for Charlotte, though the veins in her hands stood out. She must really be losing weight, Charlotte thought.

"Oh, Charlotte, it is so good to see you, " Alice said as they hugged. "Please come sit down beside me and tell me everything about North Carolina."

Charlotte told her about the church and the school, about her arrival in Sedalia, about teaching the children and how they sang, about the lessons with Mattie Nevils, about the letter that closed the school. She told Alice about how she had become a part of the community by getting most people to accept her. As she talked, Charlotte noticed some of the sparkle returning to her friend's eyes. Alice laughed when Charlotte described in detail how she had taught Vina to sew when she had such a hard time herself.

"Oh, Charlotte, you must tell your mother that story. She'll be proud of all those hours she spent with you, showing you how to use a needle and thread."

Charlotte looked down, grew serious. She stood. "I just have to stay there. They really need someone there to guide them and I've become so attached to the community." She started pacing back and forth in front of Alice. "I feel so committed; there must be a way for me to stay."

"I guess there's no secret," Alice said, "I'm not feeling well. I really wanted to go out and help you raise funds for your school, but I know several people who could help you."

Charlotte stopped pacing. "I'm so sorry, Alice. I came here with all my problems, and I didn't even ask how you were doing. I'm so rude." She kneeled beside Alice and took her hand.

"Oh, it's really nothing, Charlotte, I think I'm just tired. I've been so busy and really haven't had time to myself. George and I are going on a European cruise and I should get plenty of rest. Don't you even think about me. We have to come up with some names of people who would be interested in your school." She patted Charlotte's hand.

The two women spent the rest of the afternoon talking about their first meeting, years before, and the future of Charlotte's school. Alice told Charlotte about many people who might be willing to help. When Charlotte prepared to leave, she gave her friend a long hug. "Thank you so much for everything. I will put these names to good use."

"I know you will, Charlotte. You'll make me even more proud of you." Alice waved good-bye.

Charlotte took the names Alice had given her, studied them, and tried to decide who to see first. After the Civil War, many people who lived in the North wanted to help blacks in the South gain an education. Many worked through their church and went to the South on missionary work, much as Charlotte had done. Sometimes wealthy Northerners gave money to various causes in the South like Charlotte's school. She felt grateful for the names, and hopeful. She began a long summer of raising money.

One of the first people she saw was a wealthy businessman, Mr. Guthrie. As soon as Charlotte walked into his office she smelled the new leather and the fresh-cut roses. This place smells rich, she thought. Royal blue velvet curtains hung from the windows, trimmed with gold tassels. Charlotte fought her urge to walk over to the windows and touch the curtains. She told the secretary who she was.

"Mr. Guthrie is expecting you," the secretary said, eyeing Charlotte as she showed her into his office.

I guess she doesn't see many black women come in here, Charlotte thought.

"Miss Hawkins, what a pleasure to meet you," Mr. Guthrie said, offering her a chair. He was a tall man with a graying mustache. "Do you care for some coffee, or maybe some tea?"

"No, thank you, sir," Charlotte answered slowly. She looked at all things in the office. Everything looked big, the man, the desk, the potted plants in the corner, the clay elephant under the window. Charlotte began to feel small, like she was shrinking in the large leather chair. Her throat went dry.

"Well then," Mr. Guthrie said, sitting down behind his desk. "Alice Palmer told me about your school. Now what exactly are you doing down there in North Carolina?"

"Well, Mr. Guthrie, it's a wonderful community with people who have a deep desire to learn." As she spoke, Charlotte's throat felt better, and her fear faded. She thought of all the students who depended on her, and vowed not to let a single one of them down. Mr. Guthrie leaned back in his chair and listened to her every word.

"Just think of what could be accomplished if there were enough books for everyone, and room for more students to board at the school," Charlotte said. She rubbed the soft leather on the arm of her chair. Mr. Guthrie lit a cigar, and Charlotte wanted to cough, but instead she continued, "Not only do I want to teach the children from books, but I also want them to learn how to conduct themselves like ladies and gentlemen. I want them to learn about the finer things in life like art and music. These are important, too, don't you think?"

"Yes, they are, Miss Hawkins, and something I think our young people need a little more of today. I'm so glad to meet someone that agrees with me on that matter."

Mr. Guthrie's three-piece suit fit him perfectly. Tailor-made, Charlotte thought, remembering how the children came to school in the winter with clothes that barely covered their bodies. Mr. Guthrie wore a gold pocket watch draped across his left side.

She told him how she wanted to construct new buildings, and buy new books for all the children so they wouldn't have to share. An hour passed before Charlotte knew it.

"Well, Miss Hawkins," Mr. Guthrie said, leaning forward in his chair.

Charlotte waited, not daring to breathe. What would he say? Had she taken too much of his time?

Mr. Guthrie opened his desk drawer. "You have convinced me that this would be a perfect place for me to put some of my money." Charlotte felt a smile spreading across her face. Guthrie pulled out his checkbook. "I'll write you a check right now."

Charlotte accepted the check, jumped up, and shook his hand. "Thank you for your help, Mr. Guthrie. I invite you to please come to North Carolina and visit us in the next year. I think you'll be pleased to see where your money has gone." She turned to leave.

Walking through the office, Charlotte noticed an old piano sitting in the corner. The bench had scratches all over it, and the legs of the piano looked like they had been banged up in too many moves. Charlotte thought of the music lessons she had tried to give the students, how they sang around the old wood stove. She tried to teach them the scales and how to stay in tune as they sang, but without success. Mr. Nevils did repairs out of his barn, and he could probably get that piano back in shape.

She turned to Mr. Guthrie and said, "The students at the school would get a lot of use out of a piano like that. Since no one seems to be using it, could you please possibly think about sending it to us?"

Guthrie's eyebrows went up. Charlotte thought she had gone too far, until she saw a faint smile cross his face.

After tasting success, Charlotte felt encouraged. She went to Gloucester, on the coast of Massachusetts, to raise money. Many wealthy people took their summer vacations at the popular resort areas lining the coast. She walked from one resort to the next, speaking about her school, describing her intentions, and asking for money. Most of the hotels were miles apart, but Charlotte walked tirelessly, day after day.

One day, after finishing one of the longest walks, Charlotte decided to rest in back of the hotel she'd reached. I'm just so tired, she admitted to herself as she sat on a rock under a tree. She had already asked the owner of the resort if she could speak to his guests at lunch, promising to take only a few minutes of their time. All he promised her was that he would think about it.

I don't blame him if he doesn't let me talk to his guests, she thought. I must look a mess. She pulled the bow tighter around the neck of her blouse.

She smelled the food cooking for lunch, and realized how long ago the small roll she ate for breakfast had worn off. She stretched her legs out in front of her, and watched some seagulls diving down to the water to catch the fish that swam on top. At least they're getting something to eat, she thought.

From all around her came the sound of people laughing. They played croquette or tennis in white cotton outfits, their children chased balls across the yawn. Little girls had light pink or blue bows tied in their hair. Couples played cards at tables while they sipped lemonade. Charlotte felt she didn't belong there. As her stomach grew tighter and tighter, growling, a single tear rolled down her face. Before she could stop herself, Charlotte's tears poured, her sobs sounded to her like yells, but she didn't care. How could the people hear her over their laughter? Would they even care if they did hear her? Would it matter to them how lonely she felt? She hadn't seen one familiar face for weeks, just a constant stream of strangers, faces that might welcome her or look at her with disgust.

Her feet ached. All the walking she had done had worn her shoes down until the soles were as thin as paper. Charlotte thought about taking off her shoes and stockings and sticking her feet in the water. She thought about feeling the cool water on her toes, letting her pain drift off into the ocean, while dropping handfuls of water down her legs to ease the heat. She thought about doing it, wanted it badly, but she couldn't do it. A lady didn't stick her feet into the water. Charlotte reached down and rubbed her ankles. They were stiff and swollen from too much walking. I ache all over, she thought.

She wanted to quit. If only so many people weren't depending on her.... She looked up to the afternoon sky through the trees and her tears, turning to the only place she felt she could find any comfort. "Please, God, let me know if this is what I should be doing. I feel so alone now, please be with me."

Before she finished the last word, a woman stepped up to tell her that the owner wanted her to come in for lunch and speak to everyone.

Charlotte's crisis passed. She later wrote, "It was a moment of triumph for me, not the lunch which had been so nicely prepared, but knowing it was God's way of teaching me that He would care for me, even provide me with daily bread, if I would trust him...."

The rest of the summer Charlotte worked tirelessly and without complaining. She raised the remainder of the money she needed for the school and for her return trip to North Carolina.

While Charlotte was busy in the North, the citizens of Sedalia worked on their own to help the school. Reverend Baldwin donated fifteen acres of land and his blacksmith shop so the school could have a suitable site. The shop was converted into classrooms, with a living room and kitchen downstairs.

Mr. Guthrie did send that piano down, attached with a note: "I expect a grand concert when I come visit you. Good luck, Miss Hawkins."

* * *

Charlotte returned to Sedalia tired, but thankful and happy with what she had accomplished, and with the way others had come together for the school. She sat down to write her mother a note about all the good news when a letter came for her from Mr. Palmer. She didn't breathe while she opened and read it.

Alice Palmer had died.

Charlotte cried for her friend, but she didn't have the time to allow herself grief. Too much work had to be done. She wrote her mother, "I must do something to remember Alice Palmer. She gave me so much. Without her, I would have never gone to Salem Normal School, or had the chance to stay here with the people of Sedalia. I'm going to name my school after her and educate hundreds of students for years to come."

Six

Palmer Memorial Institute

Charlotte scraped her shoes on an old wooden board, trying to remove the red clay "glued" to the soles. How in the world do they get anything to grow in this, she wondered. It was the first sunny day they had seen all week, and red mud was everywhere, including all over Charlotte's shoes and the bottom of her dress.

"Having a little trouble there, Miss Hawkins?" Reverend Baldwin said, carrying a newly-sawed board across the field toward the building being worked on.

"It's this red clay, Reverend Baldwin. I just don't see how it serves any purpose."

The reverend smiled as he lay down the board. "Well, the good Lord put it here for some reason."

"Maybe to teach me patience," Charlotte said before she laughed.

Charlotte, Reverend Baldwin, and some of the students and parents had worked all morning, trying to fix up an old building. Charlotte had persuaded Reverend Baldwin, who owned it, to let the school use it for a dorm. The girls and teachers could sleep in the loft upstairs, and the boys could sleep downstairs. Transforming the building had become a community project, with everyone wanting to help. Charlotte smiled with satisfaction.

Until she looked around her at all the work that needed to be done. She sat down on a rock and sighed. The hot, muggy air clung to her, and she thought once more of the fresh ocean breeze off the New

England coast. Even though she stayed busy, she had never lost her homesickness. She missed having someone to talk with about books and music. Charlotte spent most of what little spare time she had writing letters home to her family and friends, and then waiting anxiously for a reply. Whenever the mail came, she always tore through it, looking for letters. She had read the few books around the community, and had even started in the evenings reading a dictionary.

"Miss Hawkins. Miss Hawkins!"

Charlotte jerked around, startled to see Mattie standing over her. "I'm sorry, Mattie. I didn't realize you were speaking to me."

A big grin spread over Mattie's face, then she laughed out loud. "Miss Hawkins, where do you go?"

Charlotte shielded her eyes from the sun. "What do you mean, where do I go?"

"When you start staring off like that. Where do you go? Back home up North, or off to someplace in those books you're always talking about?"

Charlotte pointed at her shoes. "I was just thinking how nice it would be if I could wash my feet off in the ocean water."

"That would be nice," Mattie said, "nice and cool, but all I have to offer you is some pork chop, a piece of corn bread, and some water."

Feeling the pangs in her stomach, Charlotte said, "That sounds wonderful."

Mattie brought her a plate and a cup with the food and water. While Charlotte began eating, Mattie asked, "Do you think we'll get this building finished by the end of the week?"

Charlotte knew why Mattie asked; it was time for the crops to be harvested, and she wanted the building done so her family could get back to work on their farm. "I think so, Mattie." She could tell by the way Mattie's eyes narrowed that she wasn't convinced.

"There is still a lot to do before anyone can live there," Mattie said.

She pointed at the worn boards on the sides, and the weeds growing tall at the edges of the building.

Charlotte also saw boards sagging in the middle, and mud caked on everything. She felt more worried than Mattie, but the work had to be done for the school to have a chance to succeed. The children who lived far away couldn't walk through bad weather, so if they were to attend during the winter, they needed a place to stay. The whole school year, since there was so much farm work in the spring and fall, only lasted about five months.

Just as the doubts made her head hurt, Charlotte closed her eyes and visualized the children in the dorm on a cold winter's night, huddled around the wood stove. She read to them a poem by Walt Whitman. Their eyes lit up as the magic of his words touched them and became a part of the rest of their lives. Charlotte opened her eyes and folded her napkin. "You're right, Mattie, there is a lot to be done, but look how far we've come. Thanks so much for the lunch." Even though I'm still not used to eating fried pork, she added silently. Still, I try to be thankful for whatever I get. "Mattie, don't worry about your crops. Everything will get done. Somehow everything will get done."

*   *   *

Everything did get done, and Palmer Memorial Institute opened on schedule, though the hard work continued. Food and supplies were hard to come by. Teachers and students ate two meals a day, usually consisting of corn bread, molasses, peas, and beans. Meat was seldom served. In order for the school to run, students had to do chores which included making beds, laundry, building fires in the pot belly stoves, and carrying water from the well to the dorm.

In her later years Charlotte remembered what it was like when Palmer started: "In a little white church, which was school and church combined, my life's work began. The plastering was broken, and half the window panes were out. With these crudities and its homemade log

Palmer's first school building
Courtesy of N.C. State Historic Sites

seats it seemed to me a forlorn, forsaken place, and yet those fifty-two or sixty boys and girls, barefooted and unkempt, heartened me with their bright questioning eyes, and in a little while, I forgot the isolation and hardships and lost my very soul in trying to help them."

Charlotte became involved in all aspects of life in Sedalia. Religion had always been important to her, and she helped with church functions and the Sunday School. She took it upon herself to visit families in the community, sometimes wading through creeks to get to their log cabins.

Her first year in Sedalia, Charlotte had lived in the tiny room in the loft of the church. Without window shades or curtains, she had to move her bed from corner to corner to escape the sun's rays, or to keep it dry when it rained—the roof had holes in it.

After her second year in Sedalia, Reverend Baldwin resigned from helping with the school. Charlotte needed help, so she hired Lelia Ireland, a graduate of Barber-Scotia Seminary in Concord, North Carolina. Lelia brought her own enthusiasm and energy, and helped Charlotte in every way she could, including fund raising. In 1904 the two women wrote one thousand letters by hand to raise money, earning five hundred dollars. Charlotte wrote, "Many a night, Miss Ireland and I would write twenty-five to thirty letters by hand to New Englanders whose names I had learned, and this was our procedure. We would write the letters, then take them into our little room and place them on the table and kneel to ask God's blessing upon them that they might find their way into the hearts of the people to whom they were addressed."

They used the money to lay the foundation for Memorial Hall. The building was completed in 1905.

Those first years saw hard work and changes. Challenges came in every shape and form, but Charlotte held onto her faith and mission, and worked through each one. She began to see students graduate, and go on to successful lives. In the 1907 class, one graduate became a pastor, one a physician, and others became principals, teachers, and farmers.

As Palmer changed, so did Charlotte. In 1911 she married Edward Summer Brown, also an educator. She met him one summer while she was home in Cambridge. He, like many other African-American students attending Harvard, chose not to live on campus. He came to Charlotte's mother's house, looking for lodging, and Charlotte found him there. They fell in love, and after marrying, Edward moved to Sedalia and taught at Palmer.

Within five years, suffering from differences in their beliefs about education techniques and in their ambitions, they divorced. Edward left to go teach in a similar school in South Carolina.

Charlotte helped organize the North Carolina State Federation of Negro Women's Clubs, for the purpose of helping improve the lives of Negro women in the clubs' communities. In 1915 she became the second president of the organization and remained in the office until

1936.

Charlotte wrote her first book, *Mammy*, in 1919. It was a novel about a slave who had been loyal to her masters all her life. When she grew old, her masters showed no gratitude toward her, and she died in a blizzard, still trying to serve them. The book told a heart-breaking tale about the way many faithful slaves had been treated by their owners.

By 1917 Palmer Institute had grown into four large buildings: two dorms, an Industrial Building, and Memorial Hall which contained classrooms, offices, and a kitchen. Just as the school's fortunes seemed their brightest, disaster struck. On the last day of the year, fire destroyed the Industrial Building, which included the Manual Training Department, the Home Economics Department, and the primary grades. The Commissary, the small building that contained all the produce the students had grown, also burned to the ground.

Charlotte's first reaction was to plan a trip up North to try to raise funds for the reconstruction, but Mr. Edward P. Wharton convinced her that the people of his home city of Greensboro would contribute enough money to keep the school going.

On a Sunday afternoon, Charlotte took a group of student singers and performed a concert at the Municipal Auditorium in Greensboro. The citizens of that city did just as Mr. Wharton promised and pledged more than one thousand dollars toward a new building, one that would eventually be named the Alice Freeman Palmer Building.

The *Greensboro Daily News* carried an account of the concert on Monday, January 7, 1918. "Hundreds came who couldn't find seats. All standing room was taken and scores turned away."

*   *   *

During the first years of Palmer Institute, Charlotte shared the educational philosophy of Booker T. Washington, the black leader and educator. They both believed in industrial learning. Most of the students who attended school were from the surrounding community,

Charlotte Hawkins in her wedding gown
Courtesy of N.C. State Historic Sites

and usually stayed in the community after graduation. They needed skills to lead productive lives, so the boys learned how to plant crops, raise livestock and poultry. Girls learned how to sew, cook, and run a home.

As she moved into her middle-age, Charlotte wanted to expand the students' interest in books and music. She planned to give the children of a small rural community something they could keep with them all their lives, an appreciation of the larger world around them. She wrote that she wanted to make their homes "happy intelligent centers. Where the beauty of a picture, a good book, as well as a field of corn, could be appreciated." She added as many books and musical works to Palmer Institute as she could, and the students' interest skyrocketed, just as she had planned.

The Class of 1916, with faculty in the rear
Courtesy of N.C. State Historic Sites

Seven

The Trip to Memphis

"Finally," Charlotte said as she laid her head down on the stiff pillow in the sleeper car of the train. "I can get some rest." She was on her way to the 1920 Memphis Conference, a meeting of the United Federation of Women's Clubs. This group came together yearly to discuss the issues concerning the welfare of all women, such as women's rights and better racial understanding.

Charlotte looked forward to speaking before a large group of influential women. During the past several years, Palmer Institute had grown in size and prestige until Charlotte had become one of America's leading African-American educators. She planned to stress three things in her speech to the white women. First, she wanted to urge the equal education of African-Americans and whites. All children must be able to learn the same things. She felt if both races were treated this way, they would have the "opportunity to know each other." Secondly, she wanted women to be treated as equals to men. Third, she wanted white women to support African-American women, their needs, and their families. She planned to remind the listeners of the paradox that whites hired African-Americans to take care of their children, but still didn't treat the caretakers as equals. Charlotte would propose fair wages and education to enable black women to enjoy the same type of life as whites.

Her mind raced with anticipation. How would her speech go over? Could she convince the women listeners to take action on her plan? Charlotte saw the possibilities, and she believed her speech might cause some changes for the better. Through her bed, she felt the rhythm of the train on the tracks, gently rocking her, and she knew it wouldn't take long to fall to sleep. As she pulled the cool sheet up around her, she heard talking outside her door. She started to investigate, but she was too tired to get up. That very day she had opened her school, an exhausting chore. That's why she had called earlier in the week to reserve a sleeper. Blacks usually were not allowed in the sleeper cars, and rode in a separate "Jim Crow" car, but Charlotte needed to rest before the conference.

She had noticed some young white men following her as she walked back to the sleeper. Right now though, she was too tired to care about anything else, and she drifted off to sleep.

The next morning Charlotte picked up a newspaper and started through the sleeper car, but she felt someone watching her. She turned and saw several men standing behind her with their arms crossed, the same young men who had followed her the night before. They stared through her, their eyes narrowed and dangerous. Charlotte's stomach twisted, and her palms turned moist.

Looking up as bravely as she could, Charlotte said, "Good morning, gentlemen."

They didn't answer, just stood motionless, still staring. At last one of them, a tall man, said, "What do you think you are doing riding in this car?" He stepped away from the rest and leaned down close to Charlotte. "You somebody's maid or something?"

Charlotte looked straight back into the young man's eyes. A cold rush went through her, her lips went dry. "No, I'm a teacher," she answered, trying to keep her voice from shaking.

The young man turned back to the others, still with their arms crossed. "She says she's a teacher," the man said. He laughed, and the others joined him.

His arm flew forward and grabbed the paper out of Charlotte's hands. "Teacher," he sneered, "you ain't no teacher. You people can't read, so don't even act like you can. Teaching you coloreds to read will only cause trouble. And I don't like trouble." He leaned toward Charlotte again. "Do you?"

Charlotte didn't think she could make her voice work. She hoped the man couldn't see how she trembled, as she struggled hard to maintain her dignity. She looked around to see if anyone had noticed that she was being harassed. No one paid attention, or else they ignored what was going on. Charlotte was alone.

"Don't be looking around for any help," he said, his lips clenched. Charlotte looked up into his blue eyes, eyes that should have been bright and filled with life, but instead they were eyes dulled by too much hate. Charlotte had never seen eyes like that, at least not directed at her. He didn't even blink as he spoke.

"All your kind are on the Jim Crow car. Just where you need to be, teacher. And I'll see to it that you go sit with the others, teacher." He glared at her, then kicked the door beside her. He walked past her down the aisle toward the conductor; the others fell right into step behind him. Charlotte knew what was coming.

The conductor approached her and told her she would have to move or else leave the train. Charlotte gave in since she didn't want to be kicked off. The conductor and the men marched her, like a ceremony, toward the Jim Crow car. They passed through three cars in which sat "Southern white women passing for Christians" who were traveling to the same meeting. None of the women appeared to notice or care what happened to Charlotte.

By the time she arrived at the Memphis Conference, Charlotte no longer felt frightened. She was angry! As she waited to be introduced to speak, she sat in her chair trying to control herself. She shut her eyes and took several deep breaths. Why do things have to be this way, she thought. She opened her eyes and saw all the white women, and she felt just as alone as on the car facing the hateful men. Yet, she was determined to speak to this group. Maybe she could reach them.

If anyone could somehow understand how blacks felt, it would be white women. They, too, had been held back for so many years. They knew what it was to want the best for their children and families.

Charlotte took another deep breath, and thought about how proud her mother would be if she could have been there today. Her mother would tell her that she had a chance to talk about her people, that she was about to speak for thousands of African-Americans, not just for herself. Charlotte pictured her mother sitting in the front row, smiling as her daughter took her place at the podium. She would motion for Charlotte to straighten her collar, and point to the skirt that didn't hang just right.

The announcer called out her name. Charlotte swallowed and walked forward to face her audience. She looked out at the women and recognized several faces from the train, women who had watched without caring while she was humiliated.

Mother would want me to look them straight in the eye, Charlotte thought. She began her speech. Her voice rose and fell, filling the room with stories of injustices to African-Americans where she lived. She told the audience what had happened to her on the train, how humiliating it was for a woman to be escorted through three train cars because white people didn't want to sit with blacks.

She moved without hesitation into a strong subject to be covered with a Southern audience, lynching. Blacks were often murdered this way, hung by the neck without a lawful trial, usually by a mob.

"The Negro women of the South lay everything that happened to the members of her race at the door of the Southern white woman." Charlotte's voice had never felt so strong. The women in the audience sat straight in their chairs, listening intently to every word. Their fine jewelry sparkled against their beautiful dresses. These are women of influence, Charlotte thought. These are the women who are married to men who have power to make laws. "We feel that you can control your men and stop lynching. When you read in the paper where a colored man has insulted a white woman, just multiply that by one thousand and you have some idea of the number of colored women insulted by white men. If insulting the character of white women was criminal behavior, it must be also true for black women. Won't you help us, friends, to bring to justice the criminal of your race when he tramps on the womanhood of my race?"

When Charlotte finished there was a moment of silence, then the audience began to clap. Charlotte stood before them, holding her head proudly. She felt good about her speech, felt that maybe she had made a start in the fight for rights for her race. She looked directly at a few of the women who had been on the train; they turned their eyes away. She left the podium, thinking, if I reached someone out there today, this whole trip will be worth it.

Charlotte decided to sue the Pullman Company for what happened to her aboard their train. Her attorney urged her to drop the matter to avoid negative publicity, but she was determined to make her case known. "A few of us must be sacrificed...in order to get a step ahead."

Charlotte fought hard, never backed down, and won the case. The Pullman Company paid her a cash settlement.

Eight

The 1920s

Back at work at Palmer Institute, Charlotte saw the students' faces filled with hope and excitement. Those faces inspired her, and she pursued her goal of providing the best opportunities for the students.

In 1922 the school began to change its focus from agricultural and vocational training to more academics. School started at 8:30 and went to 2:30 p.m., with one hour for lunch and twenty minutes for recess. From 3:30 to 5:00 extra classes took place, covering things like sewing, cooking, manual training, and farm and dormitory services.

By 1927 the school had become organized around the academic central subjects, with consideration for the students to develop their special abilities. Charlotte wanted every student to be able to provide for himself/herself after leaving Palmer.

Charlotte never ceased trying to spread the word about the school. She made speeches, wrote extensively, and promoted whenever she could. The *Greensboro Daily News* wrote about Charlotte: "She wanted to teach the Negro so that he might be able to more intelligently take his place in the industrial life in the South and assist in making this country richer and in lifting its educational and moral standards."

She wanted to help every child, no matter where they might be located. Her 1924 brochure on Palmer stated, "Nearly 2,000,000 Negro children of school age never see the inside of a school house. This striking fact alone makes it easy to understand why the Negroes are the highest in illiteracy of any racial group in the country."

Palmer was open to girls and boys of all ages, unlike the public schools with their age restrictions. Many older children who missed their chance earlier gained a second opportunity to learn to read and write. Charlotte helped any student who had the desire to attend Palmer, even if they didn't have enough money for the tuition.

In the late summer of 1928, Charlotte received a letter from a young girl who lived in the nearby town of Burlington. Charlotte saw the letter on her desk as she returned from having lunch with some of the new teachers she had hired. She sat down in the chair next to the window in her office, put on her glasses, and started reading.

> Dear Mrs. Charlotte Hawkins Brown,
> I am 16 years old and live in Burlington. I have heard about your school from many people. They all tell me how wonderful it is and that you really care about your students. There is no place for me to go to school here and I really do want to finish my education.
> If there may be any way that I could attend Palmer Memorial Institute, please let me know. I am willing to work for you to help pay for my expenses.
> Thank you for your time and reading my letter.
> Sincerely,
> Ruth Hall

Charlotte put the letter down and looked out the window at the magnolia tree she had planted a few weeks ago, a small tree that would bloom the following year if given the proper care. Weren't kids the same way? Charlotte thought about how lucky she had been, growing up with all the opportunities she had as a young girl. She pictured Ruth—she had seen so many like her—living with her family in a small house. They struggled so hard to stay alive they had little chance of making anything beyond poverty level. This girl has a lot to offer, she thought. She took the time to send me a letter, to tell me how much she wants an education. I have to help her. She smiled.

"Mrs. Gullins, can you please come here for a minute? I want you to help me with something." Her secretary came through the door, looking hot and tired. "Sit down, Mrs. Gullins. Here, have some lemonade." Charlotte poured her a glass.

"I just opened this letter from a young girl in Burlington who had heard of Palmer and wants to attend here. Her name is Ruth. She shows a lot of ambition by just writing this letter to me, and telling me of her desire to learn." Mrs. Gullins flashed a bright smile. Charlotte loved sharing stories with Mrs. Gullins because the woman had so much enthusiasm for the students. "I would like for you to take a trip into Burlington and find out where Ruth lives. I have an address here." She handed Mrs. Gullins the envelope. "I want you to explain to her father that his daughter can come to Palmer if he can pay eight dollars a month for her expenses. And Ruth can help in the dining room to pay the other five dollars a month."

Mrs. Gullins nodded. "I'll get to it this week, Dr. Brown."

"No, no, no. You must go today. I want Ruth to know right now that she will be a part of Palmer." She patted Mrs. Gullins on the back. "Enjoy your drive to Burlington. Take your time and do some shopping if you want."

Mrs. Gullins left. Charlotte had to appear that night in Greensboro for a fund raiser. She decided to add Ruth's story to her speech, how the desire to learn should not be kept from anyone.

*   *   *

Ruth became a student at Palmer Institute. Her father paid the eight dollars a month, and she worked in the cafeteria to pay the rest. She lived in a large dorm room with four other girls. Closets lined each side of the room, with curtains pulled to close off the closets. The shiny pine floors were swept clean. The door to the room led out into the hall; at both ends of the hall lay stairs that led down to the living room on the first floor. Sometimes Mrs. Brown called the girls downstairs to sit around the piano and sing spirituals and church hymns.

Charlotte lived in a house located between the girls' and boys' dorms.

On a cold Sunday night in February, Ruth sat in front of her mirror, trying to tie a ribbon in her hair. She had tied and untied so many times, but the ribbon still didn't look just right. She couldn't really concentrate on tying because one of her roommates, Jackie, stood beside her, trying to learn the Charleston, a popular dance step at the time.

"You know Mrs. Brown isn't going to let you do that at the Valentine's Dance, Jackie," she finally said. "Why are you trying to learn so hard?"

"I know I can't do the Charleston at the dance, but when I go home this summer I want to be able to do it."

"You know, we're supposed to be studying now. We'll both be in trouble if Mrs. Brown decides to come around or send the housemother around." Ruth pulled the ribbon into a bow for the last time. She looked at their open door to their room. The rule at Palmer was that during study hours all room doors had to be open.

"You're right," Jackie said. "We do have the history test tomorrow. I guess we better make sure we know all those queens' and kings' names." She stopped dancing and picked up her history book.

"Children." Charlotte's voice came over the loud speaker which went into both dorms. "Children, I have an announcement to make." Ruth and Jackie went to the doorway of their room to listen. All the other girls on the hall appeared at their doors.

"Children, I just heard on the radio that in fifteen minutes there is going to be a program on with the Boston Symphony Orchestra playing Beethoven's Fifth Symphony. I want all of you in the auditorium in ten minutes. Please file in, just as you do for Sunday afternoon vespers."

"It must be twenty degrees outside," Jackie said. They walked back to their closets to get their coats. Ruth couldn't help but stare at Jackie's new coat, the latest style with big cuffs and a raccoon collar. Jackie's parents owned a large bakery in Georgia and had sent her here two years ago. Ruth took out her mother's coat which she had borrowed for the winter. Though her mother told her not to worry, she still wondered what her mother had found to wear. Maybe one of the ladies her mother cleaned for had given her an old coat.

"Well, let's go," Jackie said as she pulled on her gloves. "I don't want Mrs. Brown looking out into the auditorium and not seeing me in my seat."

Ruth laughed. "I don't understand how she knows where everybody sits, but she sure does."

"She knows everything," Jackie answered. "She's just like Santa Claus."

Ruth and Jackie walked to a large group of boys and girls, all waiting to enter the auditorium. Most stamped their feet and rubbed their hands to stay warm, while their breath formed frozen white clouds around their heads.

"Everyone, please file into line," called Mrs. Jackson, the tenth grade English teacher.

I bet she didn't enjoy getting interrupted tonight, thought Ruth. The teachers always looked busy. Once again, Ruth wondered if they ever had a chance to be with their families. And when did they eat and sleep?

The line moved forward, and Ruth entered the auditorium. She followed Jackie to a seat. She saw Mrs. Brown standing up on stage beside her podium, frequently looking up at the clock.

"Children, children," Mrs. Brown said when at last they were all seated, and the students quieted. Ruth watched the way Mrs. Brown commanded attention. She smiled at the woman's grace, her dignity, her self-assuredness. I want to be just like her when I'm older, Ruth thought.

"Tonight," Mrs. Brown said, "you will have a special treat. We will hear the work of a genius, Ludwig von Beethoven. He was a famous German composer born in the eighteenth century. Tonight you will hear his Fifth Symphony. This is a special piece of work because he wrote it while he was deaf." She walked back and forth on the stage as she spoke. Ruth knew her eyes took in everything about the crowd. Ruth also understood how excited Mrs. Brown was that they would be able to hear this famous music. They might not ever have another chance.

"Even when he could not hear the beautiful music you are about to hear, he still composed," Mrs. Brown said. "He knew that was his talent that God had given him and he used it. Children, we each have our talent to use. It may not be composing music, but we do have a talent. Listen to this piece and you will be able to feel his love for music. We must not let out talents go to waste, no matter what may try to stop us. Remember Beethoven the next time you don't feel confident."

Ruth smiled. Mrs. Brown made her feel confident.

*   *   *

Confidence was a quality that Charlotte was known for. During the twenties she saw the vision of what her school should accomplish begin to be a reality. In 1927 she delivered sixty-seven speeches about her school, largely in congregational churches and eastern colleges. She sent thousands of mailers to individuals in New England, explaining what Palmer Memorial Institute was all about.

During this time Charlotte wasn't the only one raising money for the school. The students and teachers helped out with many projects, like sales and supplying entertainment. The annual concert by the Sedalia Singers, the school's chorus, raised more than three hundred dollars every year. And African-American organizations contributed heartily to Palmer, as did churches in both the South and North. Around five hundred dollars came in every year from these organizations.

One project begun by Charlotte early in her career helped donations to pour in. Vina Wadlington Webb, a student at Palmer, described what the project was like: "We wrote letters to the people listed in a real big, blue book Mrs. Brown gave us, called *The Boston Blue.* Together, we wrote twenty-five letters a night. When each night's work was done, we placed the stamped letters on a table, and kneeling around them, offered prayers that persons to whom they were addressed would reply favorably."

The hard work and the generosity paid off. In 1928, Palmer Memorial Institute celebrated its twenty-fifth anniversary with a play entitled "The Will and the Way." The cast traveled to Boston and presented the play in Symphony Hall. More than two thousand people attended. The play was about the hardships that Charlotte and the community of Sedalia endured to build the school. Charlotte loved the play, and loved that they were able to celebrate their anniversary using the arts.

During the 1920s blacks all over the country became more active in the arts, and some began to be recognized for their talents. This period was called the Harlem Renaissance since most of the recognized artists lived in Harlem in New York City. Charlotte knew how important culture was to each person, and she made sure her students knew about as many talented artists as possible.

Langston Hughes, one of the best-known poets of the time, accepted Charlotte's invitations to visit Palmer on several occasions. In one of his poems, titled, "Lament for Dark People, he describes some of the feelings of black people at the time:

> I was a red man one time,
> But the white men came.

I was a black man, too,
But the white men came.

They drove me out of the forest.
They took me away from the jungles.
I lost my trees.
I lost my silver moons.

Now they've caged me
In the circus of civilization.
Now I herd with the many—
Caged in the circus of civilization.

Nine

Charlotte's Impact on Sedalia

The cold wind whipped around the corner of the house where Charlotte stood. She knocked on the door, Mattie Nevils' door, and waited for an answer. An old gray cat curled up on the cushion of a wooden rocking chair that sat on the porch. The cat's tail swished back and forth, as though the movement helped it to stay warm.

Yesterday had been Valentine's Day, but not much celebrating took place in Sedalia. Flu had invaded the little town, and almost everyone was sick. Three elderly people had died. Charlotte had gone door to door, collecting money to help pay for their funerals.

Today she had come to Mattie's house carrying soup and blankets. One of the Palmer teachers found out that Mattie caught the flu, but couldn't rest because someone had to tend to her sick children and grandchildren. Charlotte still couldn't believe Mattie was a grand-mother. Last year two grandchildren had been born.

Growing older hadn't changed Charlotte and Mattie's friendship. They still talked and laughed together. Sometimes Mattie came over to Charlotte's house for piano lessons, or Charlotte visited Mattie for cooking advice, like her old family recipes for corn pudding or cole slaw. In fact, the vegetable soup that Charlotte now held was one of those recipes. She knocked again and finally heard footsteps approaching the door. As it opened, Charlotte gasped.

"Mattie, you don't look like you've slept in a week!"

"It's been tough, Mrs. Brown," Mattie answered slowly and weakly. "But I believe we are going to make it. I'd ask you in but I don't want you to get sick."

Charlotte nodded. "I'm fine. Vina Wadlington Webb's boy, Burleigh, drove me over. His family so far is still well. I brought you some soup and some extra blankets from the dorms. I want you to know that I made this soup myself. It's your recipe." Charlotte looked sheepish, hoping to draw a smile from her friend.

Mattie came through with a laugh. "Now, you made this soup all by yourself, Mrs. Brown?"

"Well, not entirely. I had some of the girls from the dorm come over and help me cut up the vegetables. One of them played the piano and we sang as we cooked."

"That was awfully nice of them. You tell them how much we appreciate it."

Mattie rubbed her hands on her apron. Charlotte realized how cold it must feel, standing before the open door. "Well, I guess I'd better be going now," Charlotte said. She handed Mattie the soup and blankets. "You let me know if there is anything else I can do for you."

Charlotte walked back toward the idling car, where Burleigh waited, looking out the window. Daydreaming again, that boy was always daydreaming. She smiled. He might daydream a lot, but he helps me when I need him. Since she couldn't drive, today he had volunteered. Last summer, Burleigh's brother, Harold, had teased Charlotte about not wanting to learn how to drive a car. "Come on, Mrs. Brown," Harold said, "if you can run this school, you can surely drive this car." Charlotte politely refused. Machines were strange to her, not something that interested her, and she had just as soon have someone else who did like them help her when she needed it.

This community is like a family to me, she thought.

As she neared the car, Burleigh jumped out and ran around to the passenger side to open her door. "How is everybody doing?" he asked.

"Well, I think they'll be fine, Burleigh. Mattie looks really tired, but

I think that soup will help her spirits. I do appreciate you driving me over here." She patted his hand as she climbed into the car.

"My pleasure, Mrs. Brown. Anything I can do to help. I'll be glad when it's spring again and all this sickness is gone."

"Yes, it will be nice when the flowers start blooming again and everyone is back in church on Sunday. I miss seeing everyone." Charlotte sighed and pulled her coat tighter.

Fortunately, spring came early that year.

*   *   *

One of the first things Charlotte did upon founding Palmer Memorial Institute was to involve the community with the school. She started a Parent Teacher Association (PTA), which worked mainly with the elementary department. At each meeting Charlotte took time to talk with the parents about their children. She spoke not only about school work, but also covered topics like how to keep their homes cleaner and safer for their children, home nursing, and games they could play as a family.

Charlotte took great pains to ensure the health clinic of Guilford County visited Palmer regularly so the people of the town could receive proper health care.

There was always an event taking place at Palmer, such as movies, lectures, and musical programs. Charlotte urged the citizens of Sedalia to attend with their children. She also urged all families to attend church and get involved in its programs. By staying involved in the school and church, the people of Sedalia were able to keep in touch with each other, and learned about the changing times in their community and world. Most who lived there were poor. They had no radios or newspapers to keep them updated on events. Electricity didn't come to the homes in the area until the early 1940s.

Houses were built of split rails or logs. The floors were hard, packed dirt. Heating came from wood stoves which were also used for cooking.

Many of the people who lived in the area made their living as sharecroppers or tenant farmers. Sharecroppers worked the land for a share of the harvested crop. Tenant farmers worked land owned by someone else, paying rent in cash or a share of the harvested crop. During the 1920s one-fourth of the entire South's population worked as either tenant farmers or sharecroppers. When Charlotte first moved to Sedalia, fifteen families lived there. Only two of these families owned their own homes. Charlotte wanted to see more of them gain independence, wanted them to own their homes and farms. She started a program called the Sedalia Home Ownership Association.

Through the efforts of Charlotte's association, by 1930 ninety-five percent of the families owned their own home or farm.

Owning the land wasn't enough; the people wanted and needed to take better care of their land. Charlotte realized the problem was their lack of training. To help, she started a weekly agricultural meeting held by the Palmer Institute farm specialist, where they discussed the problems each of the farmers faced. Charlotte also made available to all, seeds that had been tested for quality by her students. Every year agricultural exhibits and fairs were held at the school to let the farmers show off their best crops and livestock.

As the community took on a new face, so did Palmer Institute. A new girls' dorm opened in 1927 before the school's twenty-fifth anniversary. It was named Stone Hall in honor of Mr. Galen L. Stone, a contributor of large amounts of money. Charlotte recalled her first face-to-face meeting with Mr. Stone:

"On a morning in early spring, I approached the office at Eighty-Seven Market Street, Boston, and asked to see Mr. Galen Stone, with whom I had conversed over the telephone. I approached him by saying, 'Mr. Stone, I thought you would be interested to hear more of the school.'

"He replied by saying, 'I don't know that I will be interested at all,

Mrs. Brown. I have quite as many things in Boston as I can carry.'

"But I stayed, nevertheless, and kept talking. I saw on the wall near the desk a copy of that picture, 'The Light of the World,' and I commented on it and finally turned again to the subject of my quest. I saw that he was getting interested. He began to pace his office floor and said, 'How much money did you say you had to raise?'

"I answered, 'I am here to raise $1,100, Mr. Stone.'

"'What do you expect me to give?'

"And I, wanting to be modest, said, 'One hundred dollars.'

"He really looked at me in pity for he realized that my need was greater than I had expressed. Then he rejoiced my heart by saying, 'If you will go out of here and raise $850, come back to me and I will give you $250.'

"I went out of that office with the determination to go back with the $850, but I failed and did not go back. However, I returned to Sedalia, told my group of teachers what happened, and put this proposition to them: I believe that if I could write Mr. Stone and tell him that we would raise $250 of the money ourselves, he would give us $250.

"They readily consented and each one pledged one month's salary. I wrote Mr. Stone, who was an absolute stranger to me other than that conference, and told him how I had failed, gave him the new proposition, and dared to ask him to wire me if he was willing to accept it. Imagine my joy and surprise when in two or three days I was called to the telephone across the street to receive a message from Western Union which said, 'Willing to give money on conditions stated in letter.'"

* * *

Nineteen thirty-four saw the dedication of a boys' dorm, The Eliot Hall, named in memory of Charles William Eliot, the twenty-second president of Harvard University. Also built was Kimball Hall. This dining hall was constructed of fine brick, and dedicated in memory of Miss Helen Kimball and other members of her family who had made contributions to Palmer. By the time the building opened, the school consisted of nearly four hundred acres and fourteen buildings, all valued at close to a half-million dollars. All the buildings were steam-heated and electrically lighted, and were the envy of the community.

Charlotte stayed busy with many statewide efforts, such as the North Carolina Teachers Association. She served as president from 1935-1937. Blacks and whites still went to different schools, and the standards for black schools remained lower. Charlotte worked as president of the NCTA to improve schools for blacks, to increase salaries for teachers, and to encourage all teachers to develop every child's greatest potential. She also stayed involved with higher education, working to persuade the North Carolina Negro College Conference to raise admission standards for the state's black colleges.

While serving as president of the North Carolina Teachers Association, Charlotte helped organize the Efland Home for Wayward Girls. The home, located in Orange County, about twenty miles from Palmer Institute, was a place for young black girls to go when their lives appeared to have fallen apart. In 1943 it became too expensive for the NCTA to keep up funding for the home. Charlotte went to the North Carolina legislature and asked for support in maintaining the Efland Home. The legislature appropriated fifty thousand dollars for the establishment of a new facility for the training of homeless and delinquent black girls. The new home opened in November, 1944 in Rocky Mount, and was called the State Training School for Negro Girls. In 1947, the school moved to Kinston, and the name changed to the Dobbs School for Girls.

As president of the North Carolina State Federation of Negro Women's Clubs, Charlotte oversaw one of the organization's greatest accomplishments, publication of the first Negro Braille magazine. Previously there had been three hundred Braille magazines, with not one aimed toward black readers and their needs. The magazine stayed in print until 1968.

Speaking engagements continued to be an important part of Charlotte's life. At Berea College in Lexington, Kentucky, she gave a speech to the Kentucky Negro Educational Association, titled, "What to Teach to American Negroes." In the speech she said, "To think, to know, to aspire, as all other youths are striving to do, is now and must always be the slogan of the youth of our race." She also told the audience, "I believe that the end of all education is to teach one to live completely." Her speech stressed her belief that what a student learned in the classroom must be useful to them in everyday life.

Charlotte hated the racial bias of the South. She knew the same thing existed in the North, but she had little exposure to it during her stays there. As much as she despised the racial customs of the South, she learned to comply with them so that peace and harmony could be maintained. Once when her students gave a concert at Palmer, she arranged for the "entire middle aisle" to be reserved for "our white friends." Another time when she took her students outside the school for a concert, she asked the local sponsor to arrange ticket sales to Negroes "if you have a balcony or gallery."

Though Charlotte accepted some of the limits of her day, she never let society limit her mind. She wrote, "I sit in a Jim Crow car, but my mind keeps company with the kings and queens I have known. External constraints must not be allowed to segregate mind or soul."

The 3 Bs of Education: Nannie Burroughs (left),
founder of National Training School for Women and
Girls (later Nannie Helen Burroughs School), Wash-
ington, D.C.; Charlotte Hawkins Brown (center); and
Mary McCloud Bethune (right), founder of Bethune-
Cookman College, Daytona, Florida
Courtesy of N.C. State Historic Sites

Ten

Charlotte's Family

Carrie, Charlotte's mother, grew feeble and unable to care for herself. Charlotte moved her mother down to Sedalia so she could watch over her. At the end of each day, she spent quiet moments with her mother, talking about the events at the school, or reminiscing about her childhood.

One weekend afternoon, Carrie fell asleep on the sofa while reading her bible. "Mother," Charlotte said as she touched Carrie's shoulder. Wake up, Mother." Charlotte looked down at the deep lines in her mother's face; it seemed like only yesterday she had been a young woman, putting her little daughter on a boat to Boston. Charlotte remembered her fright of the ocean, and how her mother's arms comforted her on the trip. She looked at her mother's thin hands, so tiny and fragile. Once those hands had been to Charlotte the strongest in the world.

"Mother, I fixed you some tea," Charlotte said gently.

Carrie looked up at her. "What? I was just resting my eyes." She smiled sheepishly. Charlotte looked away to hide her own smile. Her mother hated to be caught sleeping during the day.

"Mother, I knew you wouldn't want to sleep long, so I made you some tea." Charlotte poured two cups.

"I remember when you bought these," Carrie said, reaching for her cup. Her finger rubbed the pink roses on the cream colored cup. "You were visiting us one summer and we went into Boston on a Saturday afternoon. What a grand time that was."

"That's why I brought these out. I thought you would enjoy seeing them."

"So much has happened since then, Charlotte." Carrie put her cup down and looked toward the window. Charlotte looked too, seeing outside a bright sun in a cloudless sky, a perfect imitation of a summer day, except that outside the window it really was a cold, crisp winter day. Still, the crocus leaves had started to peek out, a sign that they somehow knew the weather would soon be warm enough to allow the plants to bloom.

"Just look at what you've done, Charlotte," her mother said, drawing Charlotte back inside. "You have worked so hard to get this school started. Now look at it. You have all these buildings and have given many young people such a wonderful opportunity in life. And the students that come here, they're all so special. I feel better by just being around them."

Carrie sipped her tea and smiled. "I should have known when you worked so hard to get that silk slip for your graduation that you were going to do something special with your life."

Charlotte's eyes filled with tears. She leaned over and held her mother's hand. "Mother, you were the encouragement that pulled me through. If you hadn't fought for my education and taught me how to stand up for myself, there would be no Palmer Institute today."

Carrie reached out to touch Charlotte's hair, just as she had done on that boat ride to Boston. "Thank you, Charlotte. Here I am, seventy-six years old, and you're in your fifties, and I can still see my little girl in you. I can still see that light in your eyes that keeps you believing in your dreams."

They hugged each other a long time.

While staying with Charlotte in 1938, her mother died. They had had occasional differences over the years, but Charlotte grieved for her mother, and her friend.

Carrie Frances Willis
(ca. 1924)
Courtesy of N.C. State Historic Sites

*   *   *

Charlotte's house was named Canary Cottage, because of the bright yellow paint she picked out for it, and for the birds that roosted nearby. During her stay in Sedalia, Charlotte's mother loaned her money to build the cottage, since three nieces had come to live with Charlotte. They stayed in the girls' dorm until Canary Cottage was completed.

It had a large living room, a dining room, and a modern kitchen. Charlotte had her bedroom downstairs, and the nieces' bedrooms upstairs. Charlotte also had the attic furnished as living space for younger girls who attended Palmer. That way she could pay more attention to the girls who needed it the most.

Charlotte loved having her nieces live with her. They were bright and happy, and made laughter ring out in Canary Cottage. All three read as many books as they could find, and then discussed each one with Charlotte. She also taught them to play the piano, and act like ladies. Acting like ladies included knowing which knives and forks were used first, when to speak and when to listen, and how to maintain their dignity under pressure. Charlotte wanted them, like her students, to learn about as many subjects as possible.

The nieces worked hard at their studies, but every night, one hour before bed, they spent time in front of the fire with books, games, or music. Charlotte looked forward to that time as much as the girls did. And around holidays that hour and the other times they spent together grew even more special.

One afternoon just before Christmas proved to be extra special, in a way that none of them ever expected.

The tree sat decorated with bright bulbs and candy canes. The walls were hung with wreathes of holly and mistletoe. Charlotte hummed in the kitchen, getting out the pans and ingredients to make fudge. She walked through the living room to the bottom of the stairs and called, "Girls, come downstairs. We have everything in the kitchen ready to make the fudge."

It was the Saturday before Christmas. Charlotte and the girls had decorated that week, while Lula May came over to help with the holiday cooking. Charlotte hired her to supervise the housekeeping of the Canary Cottage.

Charlotte smiled at the bright decorations on the tree, carefully placed by the girls for absolute top beauty. The sun beams entering the window made the decorations sparkle. Charlotte had placed a candelabra in each window, and she planned to light them up that night after dinner. Strings of popcorn were everywhere. She and the girls had spent two whole evenings working on the popcorn.

One of the nieces, Carol, had almost cried every time a piece of popcorn broke when she tried to put her thread through. Charlotte laughed at how important a piece of broken popcorn could be.

It dawned on her that it had been ten minutes since she called the girls. "Charlotte, Maria, Carol," she yelled upstairs again, "I'm going to make this fudge myself and eat it all if you don't hurry up and come help." That ought to get them.

"We'll be right there, Aunt Lottie," they answered. The girls called her Aunt Lottie, a name Charlotte loved.

As the girls came down the steps, Charlotte saw the excitement in their faces. Since they hadn't come down immediately to help with the fudge, she reasoned they must be up to something else. The girls started to run down the stairs, but stopped and tried to hold themselves to a walk since Charlotte had told them ladies didn't run down stairs. Charlotte watched them, tried to think like them. They saw her looking, and Maria blushed.

Charlotte smiled. The girls must have been talking about what to get her for Christmas. She bet Maria had blushed, thinking that her Aunt Lottie could see exactly what went on in her young mind. Charlotte remembered the girls whispering a few days earlier when they had gone into Greensboro. Charlotte had admired a scarf from outside a department store window, and the girls had noticed.

"Come on, young ladies," Charlotte said, trying to mask the fact that she really did know what the girls were thinking. Yet, just as she knew them well enough to read their minds, she also knew she couldn't fool them. Maybe it was better to play along. She put her arm around Maria. "You three look like you are up to something."

"It's Christmas time, Aunt Lottie," little Charlotte said. "We may have a surprise or two for you."

"A surprise?" Charlotte grinned at them. "I would like that." The girls giggled.

They entered the kitchen, where the smell of chocolate became almost a living thing. Carol stirred the fudge in the skillet and said, "Isn't Christmas just wonderful? I wish it could last all year, especially all the good things to eat."

"I bet you'd get tired of eating fudge everyday," Charlotte said, keeping a straight face.

"Never," Maria answered. "I could eat it everyday for the rest of my life." They all laughed.

Charlotte greased the pan for the fudge, then poured the hot gooey chocolate in. Meanwhile the girls rolled out dough for Christmas cookies. Maria started to cut a bell with one of the cutters Charlotte had dug out of the attic late last night. She had wanted the girls to use the same cutters their father, their grandmother, and even Charlotte as a little girl had used.

They heard a scratch and a rustle from the living room.

"What was that?" Carol asked.

"Maybe it was just a squirrel outside the window gathering some nuts," little Charlotte answered.

They heard the noise again. Charlotte looked at her nieces, wondering if they were as sure as she was that the noise had come from inside the living room. She walked slowly out of the kitchen, followed by the girls. They quietly made their way to the living room door and peeked in.

The room looked empty. Then Charlotte noticed the Christmas tree shaking at the top.

"Maria," Charlotte whispered, "Get me the broom out of the closet. I think we have a mouse eating our popcorn."

"A mouse!" all three girls yelled together.

"You be quiet," Charlotte whispered. "Maria, get me the broom."

A moment later Maria handed the broom to Charlotte. "Now I'm going to try to get him out of the house. If you see him going near the front door, open it so he can get out."

Charlotte tiptoed up to the tree, reached down, and shook the bottom of it. The mouse dropped down through the branches and plopped onto one of the presents. The three girls screamed like animals and ran, bumping each other, into the kitchen.

The mouse ran away from the Christmas tree, with Charlotte and the broom right behind. The mouse neared the front door, but Charlotte couldn't get it open in time to get the mouse outside.

"I told you girls to get near the door," she yelled, starting to breathe hard from running. "He's more scared of you than you are of him." She chased the mouse in circles until they ended up back at the tree.

The girls' heads reappeared at the living room door, just as the mouse took off again with Charlotte in hot pursuit. This time she didn't hear the girls scream. Instead they burst into laughter. They pounded each other on the back and leaned on the wall. Charlotte stopped the chase for a minute to stare at them.

She saw they were laughing at her.

Charlotte almost yelled at the girls, almost told them to help her instead of standing there and laughing, but she considered what the girls were watching. There she was, chasing a mouse, holding a broom over

her head like a club. She took short steps when she ran, and her dress
flew behind her like the tail of a bird. She felt her face locked in the
same intent expression she had when she gave a speech. Several strands
of her hair fell down along the side of her forehead and temple.

And she always stressed to the girls how important it was to look
and act like a lady. They had never seen her before when she wasn't
prim and proper. A smile spread over Charlotte's face.

Just then the mouse stopped running, turned, and stared up at
Charlotte and the broom. The girls laughed even harder, and Charlotte
had to laugh just as hard. The mouse watched.

When she could finally speak again, Charlotte said, "All right.
Carol, open the front door. I'm going to get him out of here."

Carol crept around the edge of the living room, away from the
mouse, while the other two nieces snickered. Carol swung the door
open, and Charlotte leaped forward, swinging the broom. She swept
the mouse across the floor, and right out the door.

The girls cheered and marched around the room like a victory
parade.

"I didn't expect a mouse to visit for Christmas this year," Charlotte
said. "That settles it. We're getting some tinsel to put on the tree. Let's
get that popcorn off right now." The girls still played instead of coming
to help her. "Unless you want the mouse to come back."

The girls ran to the tree. The popcorn was off the tree in less than
a minute.

*   *   *

The three nieces' birthdays were also special at Canary Cottage.
The November 25, 1936 issue of the *Sedalia Sentinel,* the school newspaper, had this account of little Charlotte's birthday:

"On November 22, 1936, Dr. C. Hawkins Brown entertained at a
birthday party in honor of her niece, Miss Charlotte Hawkins. The party
was from eight to ten...the very interesting game *Monopoly* was enjoyed

by some of the boys and girls. The dancing and card playing was enjoyed by everyone after which we were served ice cream as a refreshment. I am sure the party was enjoyed by all."

The article was written by little Maria.

*   *   *

Charlotte spent a lot of her time with her family, but she also had to oversee the changes that took place at Palmer Memorial Institute. During the late 1930s, public elementary and high schools opened in most regions of the South. In 1937, a public school opened in Sedalia. Charlotte had a great deal of influence on the teachers hired for the new school; over half of them were graduates of Palmer.

The public high school took away almost all of the local students that had been attending Palmer, but Charlotte had anticipated this and spread her recruiting to the South and along the East Coast. Palmer Memorial Institute changed to a prep school.

Her move paid off. Palmer became known across the country as one of the finest finishing schools for African Americans. Students eventually came from every state. Most of the graduates went on to college.

Eleven

Good Manners

Charlotte sat on her screened back porch, enjoying a glass of iced tea and some fresh pound cake Lula May had baked that afternoon. She heard the sound of a musical instrument coming across the lawn. It can't be, she thought. The music came from the direction of the boys' dorm. Those boys know it's study hour and not time to be playing around.

Crickets chirped in the nearby woods. Charlotte expected that, but still she heard music. I still don't believe it, she thought. And just last week I stressed to the students how important it was for them to study for their final tests. She grabbed her sweater and started off across the campus.

Charlotte would turn sixty next month, but she still walked with the speed and determination of a twenty year old. When she felt determined to do something, she had never been one to slow down for anything. She stumbled when her foot sank into a small hole, but she managed to stay on her feet and kept going.

At the boys' dorm she couldn't tell if the music came from the second or third floor, so she started on the second. She marched down the hall, making sure all the doors were open as required during study hours. It must be on the third floor, she thought. She went up another flight of stairs, and heard clearly the sound of a saxophone coming from behind a closed door. One boy was making enough noise to disturb the whole dorm.

She pounded on the door. "Young man, young man," she yelled.

"Open this door right now."

The student playing the saxophone must have thought it was one of his friends teasing him, disguising their voice to sound like Charlotte. He yelled back, "Shut up and get out of here."

Charlotte felt her face grow even hotter. She yelled back through the student's door, "This is Dr. Brown."

The music stopped. Hesitant footsteps came toward the door. The handle turned and the door cracked open just enough for the boy to peek out into the hall. His eyes flew open wide. Charlotte didn't wait for him to open the door the rest of the way. She pushed it open and went inside, closing the door behind her. The other boys on the hall heard Charlotte's loud lecture. Some of them winced, some of them snickered.

They all studied quietly.

*   *   *

Charlotte stressed good manners to her students. She felt by learning good manners young people would become more self-confident and secure. One of the ways she taught manners was to have teas at Canary Cottage. Different groups of students received invitations throughout the school year, with Charlotte making absolutely sure every student was given the opportunity to attend. She served tea with her fine china and silver, giving lessons on how to use each item properly. She allowed no gossip, only conversations about books and classical music.

All Palmer students also learned to dress correctly. The girls wore gloves when they attended church, and their hemlines were checked. When they went to town they had to wear hats. And no matter where they were, girls crossed their legs at the ankles when they sat down.

During Palmer's early years, students wore uniforms only on special occasions, but during the forties uniforms were required on Fridays and anytime a group went on a trip. The uniforms consisted of black or navy pants for boys, and black and navy skirts for girls. Both wore white shirts, and boys wore black ties. Girls wore black chiffon ties around their necks. Both boys and girls wore maroon blazers.

Social events were important to Charlotte, the faculty, and the students. Different types of dances were held on campus. Everyone attended, including the teachers who chaperoned. Barn dances meant students danced the jitterbug—a popular step at the time—to a jukebox. The Junior-Senior Prom was held in the spring. Girls wore formal gowns, some of which were sent by airplane from far-off parents. A month before the prom, dancing lessons were held at four o'clock every afternoon. Boys learned to hold the young ladies correctly, while the girls learned to keep a proper distance from their partners. At the dances, Charlotte walked around with a yard stick, making sure all couples danced at least three feet apart so they would have room to maneuver.

Social hours, also chaperoned by the teachers, took place on Sunday afternoons. The students could talk to each other and play games. During the warmer months they ate ice cream. Senior boys were allowed to visit the senior girls in the sitting area of the girls' dorm. At other times, the students socialized in the classroom and dining halls.

Charlotte had a wooden floor installed in the gym so students could roller skate. Twice a month on Friday and Saturday nights, the school rented movies and seniors could attend with their dates. Seniors also were allowed to go to Greensboro, but only the boys could go un-chaperoned. Smoking wasn't allowed on the campus, although some boys went across the street to a grocery store and smoked.

In 1947 *Ebony* magazine ran an article about Palmer Memorial Institute in its October issue. Griffith Davis, whose sister went to Palmer, wrote the article. Griffith, a student at Morehouse College in Atlanta, Georgia, was doing an internship at the magazine. He described the social learning he found at Palmer:

"About the campus there is a certain air of culture which is a reflection of the personality of the venerable Dr. Charlotte Hawkins Brown, PMI's founder and president.... Etiquette training begins at breakfast with nine school mates who all practice the correct way to eat. The boys pull back the chairs for the girls next to them and sit only after the ladies are seated.

"After 8:30 chapel there are classes until four. Then comes study, socializing, and chores. All students are required to do two hours work daily at the school. Assignments are changed every six weeks, and include dishwashing for girls, janitor work for boys.... Students serve as waiters for a two-week period." Davis went on to say that when he visited the school, he felt a togetherness among the students that he'd never seen before.

Students also learned responsibility by taking turns running a campus store called the "Tea Room." It was a snack area, a place for the students to take a break, get a drink and something to eat. The "Tea Room" was located behind Kimball Hall, and gave the students the opportunity to learn how to run a business. Girls weren't allowed in the "Tea Room" after supper.

There were many activities in which students could become involved. The most famous was the Sedalia Singers, the talented group that became known across the country. They sang at the Symphony Hall in Boston, the Town Hall in New York City, and at the White House during Franklin D. Roosevelt's administration. Other student activities included the Sedalia Players, a theater group; a dance club; the Grace L. Deering Literary Society, named after an early teacher at Palmer; *The Palmerite*, the school annual; and *The Sedalia Sentinel*, the newspaper. Sports were also stressed at the school, featuring tennis, baseball, and basketball.

Religious life was never ignored at Palmer. Charlotte made sure each student learned passages from the bible. Everyone had to learn the *Alleluia Chorus*, for the whole student body sang it at Christmas and

Easter. A chapel service was held every morning before classes at eight-thirty; on Wednesdays, the program would consist of a minister or someone else giving a religious message. The other days of the week, the service was a time for announcements and for student groups to perform. Occasionally Charlotte would speak about her travels or some topic she felt like sharing with the students.

One snowy morning, Charlotte announced at the assembly that everyone was going to take a nature walk. She told the students to go back to their rooms and put on their heavy boots and coats. Then she led them on a walk through the woods. The teachers went along, too. It turned out to be one of the most enjoyable assemblies ever, as the adults and children alike played in the snow and marveled at the wonders of the outdoors.

Charlotte hand-picked each teacher. They came from both New England and the South. Teachers' duties included teaching classes, chaperoning students, helping with various clubs, and organizing other student activities. They were often kept busy seven days a week.

In return Charlotte made sure the teachers were treated with respect. She tolerated no abuse or disrespect from any student. One story demonstrates her absolute determination to make sure the teachers were treated honorably:

*   *   *

Mickey, the president of the junior class, sat outside Dr. Brown's office, waiting to see her. His hands were sweaty, while he felt a little cold all over, his usual reaction when he was nervous. He started taking deep breaths to calm himself, and noticed the secretary watching him and smiling. "It shouldn't be much longer," the secretary said. "Dr. Brown received a phone call right when you walked in." Mickey nodded and thanked her.

He had been into Dr. Brown's office many times, but today was different. She had been in a terrible mood since the beginning of the week, since the incident with the senior boys. Mickey's roommate relayed all the details to him. The senior boys took a trip to Greensboro. On the bus trip back, one of them cursed at a teacher.

And boy, when Dr. Brown found out!

She ordered everyone to the chapel, and told the senior boys to pack their things and get out. They were going home. If they didn't have enough money, she would pay for their trip.

It still didn't seem real to Mickey. Everyone talked about it all the time. Mickey knew that Dr. Brown had called him there today for something that had to be related to the bus incident.

He jumped when he heard over the intercom, "I'll see Mickey now." His hands felt icy.

Mickey summoned all his courage and walked to the door. He opened it and entered Dr. Brown's office. She sat behind her desk, reading some papers. He stopped and watched her a moment, trying to see what kind of mood she was in. Her face was smooth; she really didn't have many lines in her face for a woman her age. Mickey knew Dr. Brown was about the same age as his grandmother, but she looked so much younger. She must be ageless, he thought. Her light blue blouse was pressed perfectly, not a wrinkle in sight, and the dogwood brooch she wore at her neck looked nice against the blue background. Dr. Brown wore her glasses down on her nose so she could see better, and her hands were swollen a little. Mickey knew she suffered from arthritis. He walked forward to stand before her desk. She kept reading the papers. Figuring she didn't know he was there, Mickey coughed.

"I'm well aware that you are here, Mickey," Dr. Brown said with a little smile. She put the papers down on her desk. "Have a seat. You and I have to talk."

"Thank you, Dr. Brown." Mickey sat in the chair as straight as he could. He would make sure he didn't do anything improper now.

Dr. Brown folded her arms across her chest. "I'm sure you know all about what happened earlier this week with the senior boys on their bus trip to Greensboro."

"Yes, I know, Dr. Brown."

"An unfortunate incident, I might add." Dr. Brown's eyes never left Mickey, and he squirmed in his seat. "You are the president of the junior class and that brings with it a large amount of responsibility. You are in charge of your classmates, and they have made the decision to make you their leader."

Mickey waited, unsure if she wanted a response or not. "Yes, Dr. Brown," he said quickly.

"Therefore, I am holding you responsible for your classmates' actions. If anyone of the junior boys are found speaking rudely to one of the teachers, I will not send them home, Mickey. I will send you home. That's all I wanted to talk to you about today." She uncrossed her arms and picked up the papers again. "You may go back to the dorm now."

"Yes, Dr. Brown." Mickey got out of his chair, thought a minute, and added, "I'll make sure that the junior class will not disappoint you."

Mickey caught the smile that Dr. Brown tried to hide. "Very good."

As Mickey left the office, he let out a big breath he had been holding. It could have been worse, but wait a minute! He was responsible for all his classmates? He groaned. Why did he have to be elected class president? There was no way he could control all the others.

Mickey walked back to his dorm, thinking mostly about resigning as president. He knew that would disappoint Dr. Brown, and maybe that's what kept him in the office. He decided to go straight to the members of his class, even if they laughed at him, and tell them that Dr. Brown would not tolerate any more disrespect. To his relief, he found they were just as worried as he was about bringing down the wrath of Dr. Brown on themselves and their class. They didn't want to disappoint her either.

The senior boys came back to Palmer to finish out the year. Mickey never had any trouble with his classmates. He understood what Dr. Brown had done to him; she made him a stronger leader.

*   *   *

Charlotte's reputation for manners and social graces became known throughout the nation. She was a guest on the CBS radio show, *The Wings Over Jordan.* Her talk was titled "The Negro and the Social Graces." She stressed how important manners were in helping blacks gain success. She said, "Alas, in our day good manners for both races are almost outmoded. In many instances, we have lost the art of fine living. The Negro, with all his handicaps, has now the opportunity of his life to develop anew the art of fine manners as one of the means by which he may climb the ladder of success.

"The white race, having reached such heights of culture in their civilization, often times feel they can afford to go back to earlier stages of barbarism, to sweatshirt grooming, to hilarious party and dance performances.

"Let us take time, therefore, to be gracious, to be thoughtful, to be kind, using the social graces as one means of turning the wheels of progress with greater velocity as the upward road to equal opportunity and justice for all."

Representatives from *The Journal and Guide,* a popular weekly magazine published out of Norfolk, Virginia, heard the program and asked Charlotte to write a column for them on social graces. Charlotte eagerly accepted their offer, hoping to be able to not only spread her message on the importance of good manners, but also to let parents across the country see one of the sides of Palmer Memorial Institute. Her column, called "The Correct Thing," started in April, 1940. It was widely read and praised, and Charlotte earned the title, "The First Lady of Social Graces."

Encouraged by the column's success, Charlotte wrote a book entitled *The Correct Thing to Do, to Say and to Wear,* which was published in 1941. It sold well, went through five printings, and was revised as late as 1965. In the chapter, "How to Act at Home," Charlotte offered these suggestions:

> Offer your assistance in whatever work needs to be done. Don't think that you just can't wash dishes because you are a boy, or you would not dare clean up the front yard because you are a girl.
>
> Don't leave the sections of the family newspaper scattered or turned inside out when you finish reading it. Put the various parts together so that the next person can easily find and handle them.

In the chapter, "Mealtime," she covered such rules as:

> Young men, draw back the chair for the girl or woman next to you, push it under her as she sits down and then take your seat.
>
> At the conclusion of the meal, place the knife and fork across the back of the plate parallel to each other.

From the chapter, "At the Movies:"

> If eating is permitted, make the least possible noise with paper wrappings and peanut shells. If the theater is crowded, do not wait to see the picture through twice. Leave and make room for others.

With instructions such as these, "The First Lady of Social Graces" added to the manners of her race and her nation.

Charlotte gives Cookie, her grand niece, a tour of the PMI campus
(ca. 1947)
Courtesy of N.C. State Historic Sites

Twelve

The 1940s - Successes and Segregation

The 1940s were some of the most exciting years for Palmer Memorial Institute. The school was known and praised worldwide. Students came from more than forty states and several foreign countries, including Liberia and the West Indies.

And with the school's popularity came the opportunity for its students to hear some of the famous leaders of the time speak, such as Mary McCloud Bethune, and Eleanor Roosevelt, wife of President Franklin D. Roosevelt.

Charlotte had been friends with Mary McCloud Bethune for many years. They both headed schools for African-Americans; Bethune was president of Bethune-Cookman College in Daytona, Florida. She, like Charlotte, had earned her own education at a time when few blacks had the opportunity. She then taught at southern schools in Georgia, South Carolina, and Florida. In 1904 she opened a school for blacks in a rented house in Daytona, a city with a large black population. Her first school, like Palmer, stressed religion and industrial education, and became known as Daytona Normal and Industrial Institute School. In 1929 she founded Bethune-Cookman College to further the educational opportunities for African-Americans.

Bethune was a friend of Eleanor Roosevelt, and introduced her to Charlotte. Roosevelt had become known as a leader in the movement to gain rights for women and African-Americans.

In one of the greatest moments for Palmer Memorial Institute, Charlotte Hawkins Brown, Mary McCloud Bethune, and Eleanor

Roosevelt all spoke at the campus, one after the other. It was an event the citizens of Sedalia didn't soon forget.

Charlotte had no fear of asking symphonies and famous artists to perform at her school. She wasn't always successful, but there were many great performances in Sedalia. The entertainers extended from Marian Anderson, the great opera singer, to Rin-Tin-Tin, the famous German shepherd movie star.

Though bringing variety to Sedalia took much of Charlotte's time, she still traveled and made speeches. She eventually spoke in forty-seven states and Washington, D.C. She gave speeches on a regular basis at Mount Holyoke and Smith College, and the School of Education at

Charlotte poses with dignitaries and supporters at a PMI graduation. Standing beside her is North Carolina Governor Melville Broughton; educator and leader John Dewey Hawkins is top row, left.
Courtesy of N.C. State Historic Sites

Dovey M. Davis, PMI class of 1946, receives her diploma from Charlotte
Courtesy of N.C. State Historic Sites

Wellesley, usually covering civil rights' topics. Just as she emphasized
to her own students, her speeches stressed that all people were equal,
regardless of their skin color.

Yet, she constantly had to fight injustices against her own race. She
never had a personal stake in these fights, but she did all she could to
help those involved, and her help was formidable. During World War
II, a training camp for soldiers was under construction in Greensboro.
No blacks were hired for the job. Charlotte went to the local Employ-
ment Security Commission office and asked why. When she couldn't
get a satisfactory answer, she made dozens of calls to government
agencies in Washington, D.C. Her message was heard. Soon blacks
were hired to work at the construction site.

Also during World War II, Charlotte made a speech at Madison Square Garden in New York City, titled, "The Role of the Negro Women in the Fight for Freedom." She told how it made her feel to see black men fighting and dying on the battlefield just like white men, only to come home and be treated as inferior beings. She said, "...the Negro

Sports were always encouraged at PMI. This is one
of the girls' basketball teams from the 1940s.
Courtesy of N.C. State Historic Sites

woman has been through the years and is today the burden bearer of the race. Her boys in Tunisia, her boys in Australia, her boys upon the high seas, in the camps and of this country are suffering all kinds of injustices and inconveniences because of the color of their skin."

Though she admitted white women faced a tough battle for equal rights, she said, "I repeat, no white woman has ever been called on to bear what the Negro woman has borne, for added to the struggle of womanhood of the white race to gain recognition in affairs of state in America, the Negro woman has had the handicap of color, prejudice, unjust discrimination and lack of respect for her personality."

In 1947 Charlotte received the second annual Award for Racial Understanding from the Council of Fair Play. This group consisted of northerners and southerners who were concerned with the betterment of race relations.

Greensboro, along with the rest of the South during the 1940s, was segregated. Segregation means that different racial groups had to live apart from each other. There were separate bathrooms and drinking fountains for blacks and whites. Black and white children went to separate schools, ate in separate restaurants, and went to different churches.

In Greensboro's downtown there was a section of African-American merchants located near East Market Street. African-Americans could do some shopping in the "white" part of town, but they were treated differently from the white customers. Service to blacks always took second place compared to service for whites, and if a black wished to use the restroom or have lunch, they had to go to the "black" section of Greensboro, or else visit the home of someone they knew.

The Carolina Theater, located downtown, was one of the places Charlotte liked to take her students to see movies and hear concerts. Yet, the students were not allowed to go into the theater's lobby. They had to enter by the steps on the side of the building that led up to the balcony. And that's where they had to sit.

One story illustrated what Charlotte's students faced, and the way they usually reacted:

Jeanne and Lucy walked through the Gate City Department Store, laughing and talking about their dates for the prom. They headed up the escalator toward the dress department. Their chaperone, Mrs. Totton, the physical education teacher, had told them she would meet them upstairs in a few minutes to look at the dress Jeanne picked out for the dance. The two girls were having so much fun with their own conversation, they barely noticed the two white girls who followed them up the escalator.

"I want to get a drink of water before I start looking," Jeanne said as she passed the water fountains. A sign over one said "Whites," a sign over the other one said "Coloreds." Jeanne and Lucy had joked before about what would happen if they drank out of the wrong fountain. Would an alarm go off? Would security guards appear and drag them out, kicking and screaming? The kids from the North had told them they didn't have different water fountains there. Jeanne shook her head and leaned over the fountain marked "Coloreds."

The two white girls had stopped behind Jeanne, watching and whispering. One of them said, "Excuse me, but does your water taste different than ours, since you're colored. We've always wanted to know." Both girls laughed.

Jeanne always tried to do as Dr. Brown had taught her, use good manners. She stood quietly, thinking, I don't believe this. Why do these girls want to pick on me? I just want to get my dress and not have any trouble. She looked for Lucy, saw her over by the gloves.

"What's the matter," one of the girls said, "cat got your tongue?" They cackled.

Lucy heard the laughter, and walked over to the fountains. She smiled at Jeanne and said, "I got thirsty myself." She leaned over and took a drink.

One of the girls said, "I just asked your friend if the water in the colored fountain tastes different than regular water."

Lucy looked both girls in the eye. Jeanne held her breath. "I have no idea," Lucy said very seriously, "nor do I care. But since you seem so curious, please let me offer you a drink from my fountain."

"Well," one of the girls said, clenching the pearls she wore, "I have never had a Negro talk to me in such a manner. My nanny would never speak to me in that tone." She whirled around and walked off, followed by her friend.

Jeanne and Lucy looked at each other for a moment. Finally Jeanne gave Lucy a hug. "I can't believe you said that to her." She started to add she wished she had as much courage as Lucy.

"I can't either," Lucy said, wiping her forehead. "I have to admit I was pretty scared. Let's go look at the dresses. Mrs. Totton will be up here soon to help us."

They walked to the racks of dresses, Jeanne feeling glad to be away from trouble. She looked through the dresses carefully, and couldn't decide between a peach taffeta dress with a long bow in the back or a light green satin dress. She took them both off the rack. "I'm ready to try them on," she said to Lucy. They walked over to the counter where the sales girl worked.

Minutes passed. The sales girl always seemed to be busy with something else. Jeanne finally admitted to herself that she and Lucy were being ignored. Her feet began to hurt from standing and waiting. "I wonder where Mrs. Totton is."

"Excuse me, Miss," said a voice from behind Jeanne. She turned to see the two white girls who had picked on her at the water fountain. One of the girls motioned for the clerk, who immediately responded. "I was wondering if you were going to let these two Negro girls try on those dresses. Because if you were, I would like to try on the peach one before the Negro did."

She leaned past Jeanne toward the clerk and loudly whispered, "You understand, don't you? I wouldn't want to have something touch my skin that a Negro had worn."

Jeanne felt anger rushing through her, making her start to shake.

She saw Lucy about to speak. Another voice spoke from behind the white girls.

"Miss." It was Mrs. Totton speaking to the sales girl, and Jeanne saw she meant business. "Excuse me, you must not recognize these girls." She motioned toward Jeanne and Lucy. "They are from Palmer Institute and would like to try these dresses on."

The sales clerk obviously knew Mrs. Totton, who had chaperoned girls to the department store for years. The clerk blushed and walked toward the dressing rooms. "I'm sorry. I didn't see them standing there. Please try them on. You can use the dressing room in the back."

Later that afternoon, back in her dorm room, Jeanne held the soft peach taffeta dress in her hand. Never before had she owned such a beautiful piece of clothing. The peach color reminded her of the cotton candy she ate as a child when she went to the park. The white satin bow that hung in the back floated to the end of the skirt and lightly touched the lace at the bottom. She couldn't stop looking at the dress, but it also reminded her of the two white girls. They had ruined a day that could have been perfect.

Knowing that her anger only made her miserable, Jeanne hung the dress in her closet and left her room, hoping to find Lucy downstairs. She walked into the sitting room, and found her friend trying to play a song on the piano. Jeanne grimaced at the missed notes. Lucy saw her and shrugged.

"Come on," Jeanne said, "let's get out of here."

Lucy jumped up from the piano and the girls walked over to the front door. It opened before them and Dr. Brown entered.

"You two young ladies going for a walk?" Dr. Brown asked.

"Yes we are, Dr. Brown," Lucy answered.

"Do you mind if I walk with you? It's such a nice day, and I would like to stretch my legs." She smiled at the girls.

The three started down the sidewalk in front of the dorm. Jeanne couldn't understand why Dr. Brown wanted to walk with them. She felt like she should say something, start a conversation, but she didn't know what to say. She had planned on talking to Lucy about what happened in Greensboro, but how could she with Dr. Brown there? They walked on in silence, and Jeanne noticed the blooming dogwood trees they passed. She saw some of the blossoms had dropped and lay on the ground like pink and white polka dots.

They passed Canary Cottage, and suddenly Dr. Brown broke the silence. "I understand you two went to Greensboro this morning to do some shopping."

Oh, Jeanne thought, so that's what she wants. Probably to get on us for what we did. Obviously Mrs. Totton had told Dr. Brown what happened.

"Yes, Dr. Brown," Lucy answered. Jeanne saw the same thoughts she was having in Lucy's eyes. Here it comes.

"Well," Dr. Brown said, "I don't know about you, but my legs are a little tired. Why don't we sit on this bench under this oak tree and you tell me about it."

Jeanne swallowed and sat down. She tried not to, but she felt her legs begin to shake. She was frightened, and ashamed that Dr. Brown had to scold her. Just then a strange thing happened.

Dr. Brown reached over and patted her hands. Jeanne looked at her, and saw sympathy in her face. "Now, let's talk about this," Dr. Brown said softly.

Lucy began telling the story. Jeanne helped with some of the details. Dr. Brown listened quietly, occasionally shaking her head. When the story had ended, Dr. Brown sighed and patted their hands again. "It helps to talk about it, doesn't it?"

"Yes, it does," Jeanne said, "but why does it have to be that way?"

Dr. Brown shrugged. "The sad thing is that it doesn't have to be that way. Those two girls just did what they had been taught by their parents, and their parents before them. It isn't right, what they did, but they haven't been educated any other way. That's why when I go to make my speeches I emphasize to my white audiences about things like what happened to you today. They must be educated and learn that we all are the same."

Jeanne saw the pain, and the pride, in Dr. Brown's face, and she knew she would never forget that moment.

Dr. Brown touched their shoulders. "The process is just starting for equal rights and it's going to be a long battle. Some people may never change. Those two girls may never change. But slowly the change will take place. Your generation has a lot of work in front of it."

"What can we do?" Jeanne asked.

"You can do like you did today. Stand up for yourself. You have just as much right to be in that store as those two girls."

"But I didn't really stand up for myself," Jeanne said. She remembered how nervous she had been at the water fountain. Why didn't she have more courage?

Dr. Brown smiled warmly. "There will be some scary times, and I don't blame you for being nervous. You should be proud of yourself for not putting yourself down on their level by calling them names or starting a fight."

Jeanne felt a little smile take over her face. Yes, she had avoided an uglier scene, even though she had been angry and afraid. "When do you think things will change?"

"Like I said, they are starting to change now. It's a slow change, but I hope in my heart that when you have daughters, they'll be able to try on any dress in any store that they want."

Jeanne nodded, and decided she would do whatever she could to make that vision come true.

Thirteen

Twin Boys

Richard received a message during his third-period class to call home. He hoped this was the call he had been waiting on for the past two weeks. He had come to teach at Palmer just two months ago, and had to leave his wife in Boston since she was expecting twins. He didn't feel he could leave his class right then since he had given them a test, and he spent the rest of the period watching the clock count past the long minutes. He smiled, thinking, this is probably the first time these students have ever had a teacher wish more than they do that a test was over. Finally the bell rang, the last student turned in his paper, Richard grabbed his books and the tests, and raced across campus to his cottage.

He remembered how tired his wife had been the last time they talked. Please, God, let everything be all right. He unlocked the door to his cottage, threw down his things, and grabbed the phone. He knew he was nervous; he couldn't remember his wife's phone number.

A minute later, the whole campus heard the excited whooping coming from Richard's cottage.

That afternoon, Richard sat in Dr. Brown's office, waiting for her to return from lunch. He had told her about his wife's pregnancy, but it had been a long time ago, and she had so many important things to do that she might have forgotten. What if she wouldn't let him go home to see his children? What if she just couldn't let him go? What if—

Dr. Brown walked in through the door. Richard jumped.

"Well, Mr. Skeets," Dr. Brown said with a smile, "I was just thinking about you this morning. I wanted to ask if you could help me out with a project for the sophomore boys this fall."

For a moment Richard's spirits fell. He decided she had forgotten. Yet, as he watched her walk across the office toward him, some of the confidence she exuded made him feel better. She was nearing seventy years old, but her body still stood straight, her steps were strong, and her eyes never left yours when she spoke to you. Richard's excitement returned.

"Dr. Brown, I have some good news. My wife just had twin boys, and I do wish to go see them. If it is possible."

Dr. Brown reached forward and hugged him. Richard felt her small arms wrap around him, and knew they were arms that cared. Dr. Brown may have been strict with her rules, and with the education of the students, but she was a warm, compassionate woman who cared about people in a way that few others did. She released him and stepped back, smiling.

"There is nothing more important in this world than the birth of a child," she said. "Is your wife doing well?"

"Yes, I talked to her mother a couple of hours ago and she said she was fine but asleep." Richard wondered if his sentences made any sense.

"Well, I suppose you want to leave as soon as possible," Dr. Brown said.

"If I could, I'd like to catch a bus tonight. I can get home tomorrow night and spend a few days with my family." Richard watched to see if she would agree with his plans. "Then I'll have them move down here with me as soon as my wife can travel."

"Nonsense."

Richard's stomach collapsed. He looked at Dr. Brown, not knowing what to say. She continued, "I'll not have you riding a bus to Boston. I'll call the airport right now and reserve you a seat in first class."

By taking a plane, Richard could be holding his sons that very night. He couldn't believe what he had heard. He felt so excited that before he knew what he was doing, he grabbed Dr. Brown and gave her a bear hug. He realized what he had done and let go, but fortunately Dr. Brown laughed.

"How can I ever thank you, Dr. Brown?"

"You be the best father you can to those little boys. That's all I ask."

"Oh, I promise that, Dr. Brown."

"Mr. Skeets, may I ask if you have any money to go home with?"

Richard swallowed and looked at the floor. He hadn't been teaching long, and he had sent almost all his money home to his wife

Dr. Brown nodded, reached into her pocketbook, and handed him a hundred dollars. "Son, never be without money."

Charlotte in her office in the Alice Freeman Palmer
Building, doing what she did best, assisting a student
(ca. 1947)
Courtesy of N.C. State Historic Sites

Fourteen

Turning Over the Reins

As the decade of the forties drew to a close, Charlotte realized she would soon have to resign as Palmer's president. She wanted to leave the school without any financial problems. In 1947 at the forty-fifth anniversary of the school, she announced a campaign to raise one-half million dollars to ensure the future of Palmer Memorial Institute.

During the campaign, fire once again struck Palmer. The girls' dorm, Stone Hall, burned. Fortunately, all the girls had gone to Greensboro to see a movie, so no one was hurt in the fire, but only the front of the building could be saved. The girls returned that night to find their dorm, and all their possessions, gone.

Everyone at the school pitched in to help after the fire, and kept the school operating at a surprisingly smooth level. The girls called their homes and asked their parents to send new clothes. The boys moved to the gym and slept on cots so that the girls could use their dorm.

Charlotte took the fire hard, but once again her indestructible spirit prevailed. She said, "So long as I have faith in God, He will send friends to help us."

Contributions to rebuild the dorm poured in, including money from Robert Stone, son of Galen Stone, for whom the dorm had been named. The new building opened for use in the fall of 1950.

Throughout her years at Palmer Memorial Institute, Charlotte was most creative in thinking of ways to raise money. One idea was "Roll Call Day," a fund-raising competition between classes. The money raised was tabulated and displayed, so all the classes could see which of them had done the best. Charlotte planned "Roll Call Day" immediately after the Christmas vacation, so the students could ask their parents and relatives to give for the competition. The seniors always expected to win. If the juniors or one of the other classes were ahead, the phone lines at Palmer always filled with seniors calling home for more money.

The half-million dollar goal was never reached, but Charlotte did raise enough money to enable the school to operate for years to come without financial difficulty.

In 1950 Charlotte received an honor she considered to be one of her highest—The English School of Cambridge, her former high school, asked her to speak at their fiftieth graduating class. She was quoted in the *Cambridge Review* of June, 1950 as saying to the school's Headmaster, "Your selection of me for that occasion was one of the finest tributes ever paid to me, and I would want it to go down to all coming generations of Negroes as an example of fair play and interracial understanding exhibited by the principal of our Cambridge English School. Someday, I want you to honor us with your presence at the graduating exercise of the Palmer Memorial Institute."

Over the next two years Charlotte's health steadily declined. Diabetes took most of her energy, and she found the task of running the school at her usual pace to be impossible. So in 1952 she resigned as president of Palmer Memorial Institute. She named her replacement, Welhelmina Marguerita Crosson, a native of Boston. Mena, as Charlotte called her, had been at Palmer for three years, long enough to become Charlotte's most trusted administrator and successor. Charlotte felt confident she had left the school in good hands.

A huge ceremony was held to inaugurate Crosson. Charlotte gave a stirring speech, in which she told her successor, "I want Palmer to continue to be a standard school, where good breeding and good English will play a major part. I want the pupils to be courteous; I want them to be good students so that they can become an integral part of this great

Charlotte with her successor, Mena Crosson, in Canary Cottage
Courtesy of the N.C. Division of Archives and History

country, and Mena, if you preserve these values, that's all I can expect."

Crosson took over the running of the school, although Charlotte remained to help as financial advisor. They both lived at Canary Cottage.

As Charlotte's health grew worse, some of the senior girls came to visit. One day while reading out on the screened-in back porch, Charlotte saw Elise, Mattie's granddaughter, coming up the walkway. From the look on the girl's face, Charlotte knew she was excited. Elise had her grandmother's smile and sparkle to her eyes.

"You look like the cat that just swallowed the canary," Charlotte said as Elise entered the porch.

"I just had to tell someone, Dr. Brown," Elise said in quick words. She plopped down in a chair. "Charles Harris just asked me to the prom. I can't believe that he asked me."

Charlotte smiled, realizing the sight of a glowing young face full of happiness made her feel young again. How many young faces had she seen over the years? "Well, just who is this Charles Harris?"

"He's just about the most wonderful guy in the class and he always makes me laugh." Elise clasped her hands together and sighed. "Isn't springtime wonderful?"

Charlotte saw the yellow tulips blooming next to the pink azaleas outside her house. "Yes, it's my favorite time of the year. It makes you feel like a new person with all the flowers and the leaves coming out on the trees." She looked back at Elise, and knew the flowers weren't what made spring wonderful to her. The girl wanted to talk about the dance. "Have you thought about what you want to wear?"

"Oh, yes! I was telling my grandmother last night that if I got asked to the prom I wanted to go to Greensboro and find a beautiful dress. Maybe one that looks as pretty as the sky." Elise pointed up at the cloudless blue overhead. "That's what I would like, a dress the color of the sky."

Charlotte nodded. Elise leaned close to her, a smile covering her whole face. "And you know what I would like to wear with my dress?" she whispered.

"No, I can't guess."

"Something I have never had before in my whole life. A silk slip." Charlotte's eyes flew open wide. "I know it might sound silly, but I've always dreamed about wearing one."

Charlotte remembered back to a time when she carried the age and worries of Elise. The excitement from that time filtered through Charlotte's body once more. "It's not a silly thing to want, Elise. When I was a girl your age, I wanted a silk slip, too."

Epilogue

Charlotte Hawkins Brown died on January 11, 1961, at L. Richardson Hospital in Greensboro, North Carolina. Diabetes had wracked her body for many years.

She was buried under a cedar tree that she had planted on the campus of the school she had founded and given her life to. So many people attended her funeral that they had to block the road off in front of the school.

Charlotte's three nieces—Maria, Carol, and Charlotte—all graduated from Palmer Memorial Institute and went on to college. Maria moved to Hollywood, California to pursue her interest in music. She met and married the great singer, Nat King Cole. They had three girls, one of which is Natalie Cole, the popular singer of today.

Carol died as a young woman. Her daughter was adopted by Maria and Nat.

The third niece, Charlotte, now lives in California and enjoys writing. She wrote a poem titled "My Blue Chair" that describes growing up in her aunt's house.

> I wish I had my chair again
> You know the one I mean...
>
> The Blue Chair—which was in my room
> From Childhood through my teens.
> It had a coat of flaky paint
> And only had one rung
> But still, it was my fav'rite chair
> Till I was twenty-one

I used to curl up in that chair
But soon, I had to tuck
My legs beneath my growin' pains
And then just trust to luck
That I could straighten out in time to bid my friend adieu...
The one I met while reading books
Perched on my throne of blue...

The night before I went away
I sat upon my chair
And took a long last look around
And knew I'd learned to care...
This was my world, and even I
So young could seem to sense
That when I left this room I'd leave
All trace of Childishness

The years have passed and I've grown old
With memories and prayers.
I often take an evening stroll
And think about my chair...
The Dreams I found ensconced thereon
My plans to make them true
Convinced—as every child must be
The world's just made for you.

Each child had his own fav'rite spot
Where he can go and be
A king...a Queen or Captain of a
Ship that sails the sea
But what he finds by way of dreams
For deeds grow out of thoughts

So look back to your childhood dreams
You'll find the reason there.
You are what you've become
Because of your blue chair.

Palmer Institute continued under the leadership of Miss Crosson. She brought many new program to the school, including a work-study curriculum. This allowed students from different ethnic groups to work, live, and study together.

Miss Crosson tried to help the students who didn't have the opportunity to attend college by holding "Upward Bound." This summer program provided these students the chance to take courses such as art, music, grammar, and literature.

For several years, Palmer supported a European Seminar, a program that allowed students and teachers to travel to England, France, Spain, and Italy. In addition, the school provided scholarships for selected students from Africa to attend Palmer. After graduation, these students returned to their native countries to teach.

The last years of Palmer Memorial Institute were affected by integration. For the first time, blacks were allowed to attend Southern public schools. Since many parents didn't want to send their children away for an education, the new integrated schools caused a lower enrollment at Palmer, and subsequent financial problems.

Fire struck the school one last time on February 15, 1971. The Alice Freeman Palmer Building burned, which meant the loss of classrooms, the library, the administrative offices, and the auditorium. The fire plus the financial burdens forced the school to close.

In November, 1971 the announcement was made that Bennett College, a private black institution in Greensboro, would take over the Palmer site.

In November, 1987 the remaining buildings and grounds of Palmer Memorial Institute opened to the public as a North Carolina State Historic Site, honoring Charlotte Hawkins Brown. It was the first such site to honor an African-American.

For almost seventy years the ideas of Charlotte Hawkins Brown lived on a campus in rural North Carolina. Her courage, determination, foresight, and compassion touched people all over the world. Her spirit still lives more than thirty years after her death in her former students, teachers, and those privileged enough to meet her.

Charlotte Hawkins Brown with a statue of Alice Freeman Palmer
Courtesy of the N.C. Division of Archives and History

INDEX

Photo by Anette Hall

Diane Silcox-Jarrett grew up in Roanoke, Virginia and Burlington, North Carolina. She graduated from Elon College in 1981. She worked as news director for a radio station, and for the state of North Carolina, writing speeches for the governor and other state officials. She has served as a creative writing tutor and an instructor at writers' workshops. She currently lives near Raleigh, North Carolina with her husband, Alex, and her son, Daniel.